Writing Skills

A problem-solving approach for upper-intermediate and more advanced students

Norman Coe, Robin Rycroft and Pauline Ernest

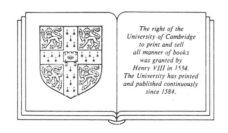

The right of the
University of Cambridge
to print and sell
all manner of books
was granted by
Henry VIII in 1534.
The University has printed
and published continuously
since 1584.

Cambridge University Press
Cambridge
New York   Port Chester
Melbourne   Sydney

Published by the Press Syndicate of the University of Cambridge
The Pitt Building, Trumpington Street, Cambridge CB2 1RP
40 West 20th Street, New York, NY 10011, USA
10 Stamford Road, Oakleigh, Melbourne 3166, Australia

© Cambridge University Press 1983

First published 1983
Ninth printing 1989

Book designed by Peter Ducker and Geoff Green
Illustrations by Chris Evans, Jim Haylock and Peter Kneebone

Printed in Great Britain
at the University Press, Cambridge

ISBN 0 521 28142 3 Student's Book
ISBN 0 521 28143 1 Teacher's Book

BS

Contents

To the student

This book concentrates on the skills that you need when you write in English. When you listen, speak, read or write, you need a knowledge of English vocabulary and grammar; these aspects of language are not specific to writing, and it is not the main aim of this book to improve them. Our main aim is to help learners to put sentences together so that the things that they write will be easy to read and understand.

Here are some of the reasons why a written piece is sometimes difficult to understand:

1 The ideas are not in an **order** that easily makes sense.

2 The ideas are not grouped together into distinct **paragraphs**.

3 The writer does not begin the piece – or paragraph – with an **introduction** that starts the reader in the right direction.

4 The writer does not end the piece – or paragraph – with a **conclusion** that sums up the point he or she wants to make.

5 The **relation** between the ideas is not clear because the writer has not used words like *although*, *for example*, *on the other hand*, and so on.

6 The writer's **attitude** is not clear; is he or she, for example, describing, suggesting or criticising something?

7 The piece contains ideas that are **not relevant** to what the writer wants to express.

8 The sentences do not have clear **punctuation**; there are commas (,) and full stops (.) without any good reason.

The material in this book practises all these specific aspects of writing. Obviously, different learners will vary in their strong and weak points, and they will therefore need to concentrate on different aspects. With the material in this book you are free to do this; you can vary the order in which you do the practices so as to suit your specific needs.

We believe that students learn a lot by working together in groups to solve a problem or make a decision. We feel that learners should share their knowledge, compare their opinions, and discuss their ideas in small groups before going on to classwork or individual work. The instructions for each exercise include suggestions about ways of working with the material. However, these are only suggestions, and different teachers and classes will adjust them to their own ideas and circumstances.

1 Informal letters

1.1 PUNCTUATION

Notice the use of capital letters in the following expressions:

1 Mrs Ashley, Mr Brown, Mr and Mrs Thompson, Lady Grey, Sir Geoffrey Land, Dr James, Professor Ayer, etc.
2 the Foreign Secretary, the Minister of Finance, the Archbishop of York, etc.
3 Oxford Street, Hyde Park, Trafalgar Square, Redhill Gardens, etc.
4 Lake Windermere, the River Thames, Mount Everest, etc.
5 Monday, Tuesday, etc.; January, February, etc.; Christmas, Easter, etc.; Christmas Eve, New Year's Day, etc.
6 French, English, Spanish, etc.; Frenchman, Englishman, Spaniard, etc.
7 the Tate Gallery, the Museum of Modern Art, the Ritz Hotel, etc.

Now, working individually, indicate where you need capital letters in the following sentences. Then compare your answers with those of others.

8 was professor blunt working for the queen of england?
9 the british prime minister met the german foreign minister for talks.
10 is lake geneva near mont blanc?
11 on thursday we're going to the museum of natural history.
12 the suggestion was made by captain jones on behalf of general taylor.
13 is dr spock american or canadian?
14 last year good friday was on april 1st.

1.2 SCRAMBLED SENTENCES

The following sentences go together to form a complete letter, but they are in the wrong order. Working in groups of two or three, put them in the right order, and decide how the words and phrases underlined help to link the text together. Then compare your answers with those of other groups.

Dear Dorothy,

a) <u>But</u> when we started eating, the noise died down.

b) As you may remember, it was Rosemary's birthday <u>last Saturday</u>, and she wanted to do <u>something</u> different.

c) (<u>You remember it, don't you?</u> Just beside the old castle.)

d) Well, <u>nothing more to tell you</u> just now; <u>hope to see you at</u> Christmas.

e) <u>I mean,</u> life goes on as always, and nothing special seems to happen.

f) Fortunately, there was a bright moon, so we were able to <u>make</u> our way <u>there</u> without much trouble.

g) It was <u>then</u> that we suddenly became aware of the stillness of the night, and although it sounds odd to say so, the silence seemed even louder than the noise we had been making before.

h) <u>Thank you very much for your letter,</u> which arrived this morning.

i) <u>All in all,</u> it was an unforgettable experience – I'm sure Rosemary's picnic will be talked about for some time.

j) It was really my turn to write, <u>as you say,</u> but I seem to have so little news these days.

k) As you can imagine, there was a great deal of messing about <u>when we got there</u> – people shouting and chasing each other around, and so on.

l) Last weekend was fun, <u>though.</u>

m) <u>Well, anyway,</u> we all met at the Red Lion, had a few drinks there, and then went on down to <u>the wood</u>.

n) <u>Instead of the usual party at home</u> she decided to have a midnight picnic in Glover Wood.

Love,

Jenny.

1.3 LINKING WORDS AND PHRASES

In the following letter the linking words and phrases are missing. Working in groups of two or three, choose the most appropriate phrase from the ones given below. Then compare your answers with those of other groups.

Dear Harry,

Remember that I told you I was trying to get a job at ICTL? (1) ...., I finally managed to get one! Of course, I haven't been working there long, (2) .... I can already tell that it's a wonderful place to work. All the staff, (3) .... the directors, are very friendly with everybody, and (4) ...., they have marvellous facilities for the employees. (5) ...., there's a bar and gym, and lots of other things.

I'm called the Safety Equipment Officer. It (6) .... sound like an impressive title, but it's not a very accurate description of what I do. My main job is to provide protective clothing, (7) .... overalls, helmets, and so on. I estimate what the different departments will need, and (8) .... I order it from the suppliers. (9) .... I make sure that the various departments have everything they want. (10) ...., stationery is also my responsibility. (11) ...., I have to supply all the offices with paper, envelopes, and so on. I find the job very interesting (12) .... I get the chance to go all over the factory and to meet everybody. (13) ...., the pay is a lot better than in my old job.

(14) ...., that's my news. What about yours? Drop me a line when you have time. Regards to your family, and best wishes to you.

Terry

---

1 a) Then   b) Well   c) And
2 a) but   b) because   c) so
3 a) until   b) and   c) even
4 a) so   b) what's more   c) on the other hand
5 a) For instance   b) However   c) Even
6 a) can   b) could   c) may
7 a) such as   b) namely   c) as
8 a) then   b) after   c) so
9 a) By the way   b) Anyway   c) In this way
10 a) However   b) Although   c) But
11 a) Secondly   b) In other words   c) Also
12 a) why   b) because   c) then
13 a) Besides   b) Beside   c) On the other hand
14 a) At the end   b) Anyway   c) After all

Each of the following sentences has a blank where there should be a linking word or phrase. Put in one of the above words and phrases so that the relation between the two statements is made clear.

15 The pay and conditions are very good. ...., it's only five minutes' walk from where I live.

16 I didn't apply for the job .... I didn't think I had much chance of getting it.

17 A lot of professional groups, ... doctors and lawyers, have strong associations that protect their members' rights.

18 The hours are short, the pay's excellent, and the people I work with are very nice. ...., it's a great job.

19 You .... think it's boring, but in fact it's very interesting.

20 All my relatives were at the wedding, ... my cousins from Australia.

21 At first I didn't feel happy with so much responsibility. ...., now I feel quite confident that I can manage.

22 There are several things that make it a nice place to live. ...., there's a park right across the road.

1.4   ATTITUDE WORDS AND PHRASES

The blanks in the following letter must be filled with words and phrases that bring out the writer's attitude to what he is saying. Working in groups of two or three, choose the most appropriate expression from the ones given below. Then compare your answers with those of other groups.

My dear Francesca,

Thank you very much for your letter. (1)_____ [Naturally], it makes an old uncle very happy to know that his niece is interested in what he thinks about her ideas and plans. (2)_____ [To my surprise], you are thinking of leaving home. (3)_____ [Frankly], I must say that I think it would be a very unwise thing to do.

Fran, I know that you are a very sensible girl, and I also know that, (4)_____ [presumably], your parents have brought you up to think for yourself. In your 'open' family you will have heard all the arguments for and against this sort of thing many times and, (5)_____ [perhaps], you won't be interested in hearing them again, least of all from me. Nevertheless, I really must say something: what you are thinking of doing could make you (and everyone else) very unhappy.

You say that you find school boring, and that what you do there is irrelevant. (6)_____ [Quite likely], I agree with you, but (7)_____ [obviously], if

8

you want to do anything with the rest of your life, you have got to keep going just a little bit longer — at least until you're got some paper qualifications. Without them you won't be able to do anything at all. (8)_____, you will have thought about these things, but I wonder if you have considered how really serious they are.

Then, (9)_____, you say that you're going to live with your boyfriend in London! As far as I remember, he hasn't even got a job, has he? What on earth are you going to live on? Life on the dole might be bliss for a few months, but I can assure you that it won't last for much more. (10)_____, just think about it — you're a bright, intelligent girl. Just how long do you think you could be happy vegetating with an unemployed motor mechanic? You and I really need to have a serious talk together.

So, Fran, please come and see me before you finally decide. If anything awful ever happened to you, I'd never forgive myself.

Fondest love, as ever,

Uncle Patrick.

1 a) Naturally   b) Perhaps   c) Surely
2 a) In my opinion   b) To my surprise   c) Actually
3 a) Fortunately   b) Frankly   c) Undoubtedly
4 a) honestly   b) presumably   c) quite properly
5 a) of course   b) perhaps   c) seriously
6 a) Quite likely   b) Unfortunately   c) Broadly speaking
7 a) to my surprise   b) obviously   c) eventually
8 a) Undoubtedly   b) To be frank   c) Unfortunately
9 a) generally   b) actually   c) to my surprise
10 a) Seriously   b) Of course   c) Naturally

1.5   REPORTING WORDS

There are two reported speech versions of the following direct speech. Working in groups of two or three, decide which you prefer and why. In particular consider the role of the reporting word blame. *Then discuss your conclusion with other groups.*

'Don't talk to me about the kitchen,' said Tom. 'It was Eve who got everything out, and then spilt things all over the place.'

a) Tom blamed Eve for the mess in the kitchen.
b) Tom told me not to talk to him about the kitchen. He said that it had been Eve who had got everything out, and had then spilt things all over the place.

Now report the following items of direct speech, choosing in each case one of the reporting words given. Then compare your answers with those of others.

praise; state; suggest; ask; think; explain; call; insist; order; advise.

1 'You walk straight down this road until you get to a big church on the left,' said Angela. 'Then you turn right, walk along for about a hundred yards, and you'll see the post office on the left.'
2 'Listen, Dick. You really ought to write and explain what's happened,' said Mrs Jones. 'In fact, if I were you, I'd write the letter straightaway.'
3 'You're a fool, Brian,' said Sara.
4 'You realise, of course, Bill,' Penny said, 'that in this weather it would probably make more sense for us to go by train. What do you think?'
5 'If I've told you once, I've told you a dozen times: somebody must pay for the broken window,' said the young lady.

Now choose two or three of the reporting words that you have not so far used; write examples of direct speech and reported speech to illustrate the use of these words.

1.6 PARAGRAPH COMPLETION

In the following letter the first two paragraphs are complete, but the next three are progressively less complete. Working in groups of two or three, complete the third and fourth paragraphs with sufficient information to explain the sentence that introduces them, as in paragraph two. You must invent the whole of the fifth paragraph, starting with the phrase given.

Dear Patty,

Thank you for your letter. It was very nice to read all your news, and it was great of you to invite us all to come over for Christmas. Unfortunately, I really don't think we'll be able to take you up on it – and for so many reasons.

For a start, I just don't think that I could get away from the office. I know I really should take a break, but it's impossible at the moment. We're having a lot of trouble with that new rolling mill I told you about, and what's more, the engineers' union want a 25% rise. As you know, times aren't too healthy on the sales side, so the negotiations will no doubt take time.

Another thing is that Charlie wants to go and stay with these friends of his in Norway. You perhaps remember

Also, Sally's talking about moving to London, and you can imagine what <u>that</u> would involve.

Last but not least,

So really, what with all of the family likely to be away for some or all of the time, I don't think we'd be very good company for you. I do hope you understand, and that we'll be able to come and see you early in the New Year.

Love from all the family,

Candice

1.7   TEXT COMPARISON

Working in groups of two or three, decide which of the following letters you prefer and why. Then discuss your decision with other groups. Finally, rewrite the letter you did not like.

Dear Aunt Nellie,
        I have just started work. I'm going to tell you about my experiences.
    I'm working in an office. It is an insurance company. There are forty other people in the office. I am a typist here. I type letters mostly. My boss is called Mr Merriam. He's the manager of the Claims Department. He gives me my work. When I have typed it, I give it back to him. He's very kind to me.
    Some of the people in the office are very nice. Some are very rude, some are very noisy, and some are very funny. I have made friends with a girl called Susan. She's a typist too. She doesn't work for Mr Merriam. She works for Mrs Jones. Mrs Jones is the manager of the Accounts Department. She is very nice.
    The work is easy. As you know, I have been trained to type, so typing is easy for me. The office is very clean. It is very modern, too. But the atmosphere is strange. It is difficult to get used to the atmosphere.
    It is simple to travel from my flat to the office. I get a number 26. I change at Bidlam Square. I get a number 12 from there. It takes about 20 minutes. I have lunch in a cafe with Susan. It costs about a pound. It's quite good value.
        Love to Uncle Ernie (and the budgie!)

Jennifer

Dear Aunt Dorothy,

Well, here I am at University for the first time, and I must say it isn't what I expected, but I think I'm beginning to settle down and make friends.

There are about a hundred other people in my class, and I think I must be about the youngest, but I don't feel out of place. I've made good friends with my tutor already; I write essays for him every week, and he's always very kind to me when we meet to talk about my work.

There are all kinds of different people in the university, from the very friendly to the very hostile. But I've met a girl called Sally who's really wonderful. She isn't in my faculty, though. She's doing medicine, but we meet every day for lunch, and we sit talking about life for hours.

My flat is very small, but it's warm and comfortable. It's also very close to the university, so it only takes me a few minutes to walk there, and I can get a bus right to the door if it's raining.

Well, I really must go now because Sally and I are off to lunch. I promise I'll write again as soon as I have a moment.

Love to all the family,

Rachel

1.8   TEXT BASED ON A CONVERSATION

Read the following letter. Then, working in groups of two or three, write a similar letter based on the conversation below.

Dear Mother and Father,

This is just a short note to let you know that Pamela and I are both very well, and we hope you are, too. Unfortunately, I've got some rather bad news. I've had a slight accident on my motorbike. There's no need to worry — absolutely nothing to worry about at all. Nobody was hurt, and it wasn't even my fault.

Anyway, here's how it happened. We were on our way to visit Joe and Rosie at the seaside. It was Pamela's turn to drive and, as you know, she's very careful, but suddenly a car pulled out from a side-road without looking, and the bike skidded as Pamela braked. The road was a bit wet, you see. We hit the car in the middle of the road, and we were both thrown off.

Luckily, we weren't really hurt at all. The driver of the car was very angry, but we were absolutely furious, and we started yelling at him. In the end, he backed down and admitted that it had been his fault entirely. There were several witnesses anyway, so he couldn't really have denied it.

After quite a bit more discussion, and thanks to the intervention of one of the witnesses, we managed to persuade the driver to sign a statement admitting full responsibility. I don't know why he did it; I know I would never sign anything like that without asking a lawyer, but I suppose he felt guilty, and he realised he was very lucky it hadn't been worse.

Anyway, as I say, there's nothing to worry about, because we are both perfectly fit and well. We'll probably come and see you towards the end of the month. We'll have to come by train because the bike's going to be in the garage for some time!

Love to the rest of the family,

Ted

J: Look out!!

K: Oh, hell! What a mess!

J: But didn't you see the kerb, you bloody idiot?

K: No, of course, I didn't see the kerb. If I'd seen it, I wouldn't have run into it, would I?

J: All right, don't start shouting at *me*. You're the one who's just smashed my car up.

K: Look, let's take it easy for a moment, shall we? Have you got a fag?

J: Here.

K: Thanks. I suppose we'd better go and see what the damage is.

J: I just can't understand why you had to drive up onto the kerb at fifty miles an hour on a perfectly straight road.

K: Look. I'm very sorry about it, and I'll pay for all the damage and all that, but it won't help if you're going to start nagging at me. It isn't a perfectly straight road, for a start. It's a winding country lane, and you may have noticed that it's almost midnight, and there's practically no lighting. So visibility isn't what you'd call optimum.

J: All right. Calm down. I'm just upset about my car. That's all.

K: Well, you're not the only one that's upset, if that's any consolation. Anyway, let's go and have a look, eh?

J: Can we move it?

K: I think so. The wheels are all right. We've just got to try and pull this front wing away from the wheel. Can you give me a hand?

J: Well, I don't think I should. Remember my back's a bit funny these days.

K: Honestly, you are the limit. Fine help you are in a crisis! Well, in that case you'd better try and stop another car because I can't do it by myself.

J: Another car at this time of night? You'll be lucky!

K: Well, you'd better go and try to find a phone, then. That is, if you think your back will stand lifting the receiver.

J: O.K., there's no need to be sarcastic. I'm off.

K: And while you're there, you'd better ring Carol and say that we might be a bit late. Be as quick as you can. Now, I wonder if I can pull this away on my own. Oh, hell. Well, that's that. At least it's not touching the wheel now.

(Ten minutes later)

K: Ah, you're back. Well, off we go!

J: Wait a minute! Where's the wing?

K: On the back seat. I'm afraid it fell off while I was trying to straighten it.

J: Oh, hell! Well, I suppose we can at least get on our way.

K: That's the spirit! You'll see. Tomorrow you'll have forgotten all about it.

1.9 TEXT BASED ON VISUAL INFORMATION

Look at the letter and the map that goes with it. Together they explain how to get to Joe's house. The end of the letter is missing. Working in groups of two or three, complete the letter, giving Tim as many helpful details as possible. Then write a letter explaining how to get from Raby Village to Chacklow Hall.

Dear Tim,

I'm very pleased to hear that you have finally decided to come here for Christmas. I think I'd better explain the route to you in some detail because it isn't easy unless you've done it before. I suppose you'll be able to find your way to the Birkenhead end of the tunnel; that bit's straightforward.

Now, when you come out of the tunnel, the road divides into two. The left fork goes down to the docks. You should take the right fork unless, of course, you feel like going to have a look at the ships! About a hundred yards further on you'll pass a picturesque old clock tower on the left. Immediately after that take the turning on the right, or otherwise you'll be on your way to the river again. The road passes through a wood and gradually bends to the left.

At the end of the wood you'll see a long straight road in front of you. That's where you have to turn right. Follow the road up to the T-junction at the top, and turn left along Mount Road. This is the main road that will take you all the way to Clatterbridge. Follow this road past the beacon on the right and

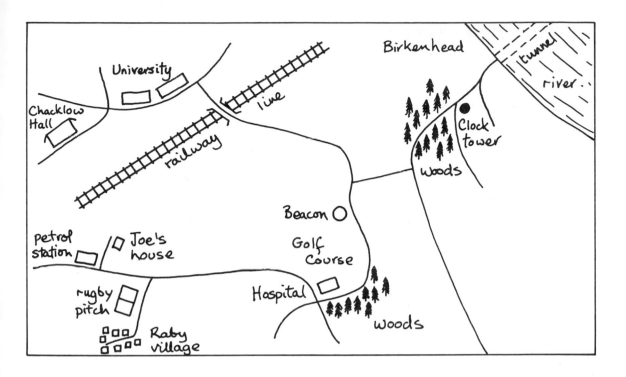

1.10   IDEAS FOR LETTERS

Choose one of the following topics, or any other topic that interests you, and write a letter to a friend or close relative. Begin and end the letter in a way suitable to the person you are writing to.

a) An English friend wants to learn your language (or another foreign language). Write a letter detailing your experience in language learning, and explain what you think is the best way to go about it.
b) A letter about an unusual party, visit or trip. (Compare 1.2.)
c) A letter about a new job or a new course of studies. (Compare 1.3 and 1.7.)
d) A letter to someone who wants to do something unusual or socially unacceptable. (Compare 1.4.)
e) A letter explaining why you and your family or friend(s) cannot accept an invitation. (Compare 1.6.)
f) A letter explaining an unexpected absence, or something else unexpected.
g) A letter about an accident, but not necessarily a traffic accident. (Compare 1.8.)
h) A letter about an argument that you have had.

2 Formal letters I

2.1 PUNCTUATION

Notice the use of the apostrophe (') in the following expressions:

It's mine.   You're wrong.   He can't come.   We'd better wait.
Mary's sister.   The children's toys.   All the students' names.

Now working in groups of two or three, put in an apostrophe where one is necessary in the following sentences:

1   I think its an elephant, but its so far away I cant see its trunk.
2   Johns brothers wife went to the grocers for us.
3   The womens changing room is opposite the mens.
4   The Smiths provided the food, and the Jacksons organised the transport.
5   Two wrongs dont make a right.
6   This car cant be my parents because theirs is quite old.

Now, working individually, put in an apostrophe where one is necessary in the following sentences:

7   Peter asked Jennys father for all the customers addresses.
8   The girls entrance used to be separate from the boys; now theres only one entrance for everybody.
9   She wont go to the dentists because its too late.
10 Whats the sense in saying its Jacks?
11 My skis are new; hers are my mothers old ones.
12 Its exact translation is somewhat difficult, isnt it?

2.2   SCRAMBLED SENTENCES

The following sentences go together to form a complete letter, but they are in the wrong order. Working in groups of two or three, put them in the right order, and decide how the words and phrases underlined help to link the text together. Should the letter be divided into paragraphs? If so, where? Compare your answers with those of other groups.

```
                                              Bartler House,
                                              Firs Hill,
                                              Hampstead,
                                              London.
                                              NW3

1 August 1982              Ref. no. BZ 463


        Dear Sir or Madam,
```

a) He would be perfectly happy <u>if I accompanied the family</u> in my accustomed position.

b) <u>Moreover,</u> on numerous occasions I have had to take on the duties of the housekeeper, since the lady who has occupied this post has had several prolonged bouts of illness.

c) I am single, 34 years of age, and I trained at the Cordon Bleu School in Finchley from 1970 to 1973.

d) My work with the Bartler family has always been interesting and rewarding, and I personally would not have chosen to move.

e) <u>This explains why</u> I am now seeking another post in this country.

f) <u>With reference to your advertisement in The Times of 30 July,</u> I should like to apply for the post of cook/housekeeper.

g) I enclose three references and a full curriculum vitae as requested, and <u>I look forward to hearing from you</u> at your earliest convenience.

h) My duties <u>here</u> have included general supervision of the six kitchen staff, as <u>well</u> as personal preparation of special dishes for banquets, formal dinners etc.

i) I <u>therefore</u> feel confident that I can combine the two activities quite adequately if necessary.

j) I, <u>on the other hand,</u> have no wish to leave Britain permanently.

k) <u>On finishing my training,</u> I took up the position of cook with Lord Bartler, and I have been with him ever since.

l) <u>However,</u> Lord Bartler is planning to leave active political life and settle in India.

```
        Yours faithfully,

        Doris Winterbottom.

        (Miss) D. J. Winterbottom.
```

2.3 LINKING WORDS AND PHRASES

In the following sentences the linking words and phrases are missing. Working in groups of two or three, decide which of the words given would be possible. Note that in some cases more than one of the words given may be possible. Then compare your answers with those of other groups.

1 We are writing to you .... clarify certain confused points.
   a) to   b) in order to   c) so as to   d) for

2 Our reply has been delayed .... the recent postal strike.
   a) because of   b) owing to   c) for   d) by

3 These matters are difficult to deal with in writing. .... we feel that it would be better for us to have a meeting.
   a) This is why   b) That is why   c) This is because   d) Consequently,

4 I am sending you my curriculum vitae, as well as other information, ... you will have a chance to study it before our interview.
   a) so that   b) because   c) for   d) since

5 Unfortunately, your letter arrived after the final date for applications. .... we cannot consider you for the post.
   a) As a result   b) That is because   c) Consequently   d) For this

6 .... you are an import-export company, you will no doubt be pleased to know that I speak several foreign languages.
   a) For   b) Since   c) As   d) Because of

7 I have had no regular work during the last year .... a persistent illness.
   a) because   b) owing to   c) for   d) because of

8 You suggest a visit in the first week of June. .... June 2nd is a public holiday in our country, we would like to suggest the second week instead.
   a) For   b) Because   c) Unfortunately   d) Since

9 Most companies take their holidays in August. .... there is little chance of much work being completed then.
   a) So   b) Therefore   c) Thus   d) So that

10 I am enclosing a photocopy of the letter .... you can judge its tone for yourself.
   a) so that   b) in order for   c) because   d) since

Complete these emails with some bad news.

The good news is that we're on holiday.	The bad news is that I have an exam next week.
The good news is that I've met a wonderful girl (boy).	The bad news is that ...
The good news is that my parents are away on holiday.	The bad news is that ..
The good news is that I have a new motorbike.	
The good news is that my sister gave me her mobile phone.	
The good news is that	

2.4   ATTITUDE WORDS AND PHRASES

The blanks in the following letter must be filled with words and phrases that bring out the writer's attitude to what he is saying. Working in groups of two or three, choose the most appropriate suggestion from the ones given below. Then compare your answers with those of other groups.

Dear Sir,

I have pleasure in informing you that your application to stage a series of World Cup matches at your ground has been provisionally accepted by the Arrangements Committee. (1) _____, I think you have been fortunate, since there were many other clubs interested in obtaining this concession. (2) _____, your ground is not totally suitable for the purpose, but (3) _____, I am sure that you will make every effort to remedy such shortcomings as there may be. (4) _____, you will derive great benefit from this opportunity, since your club will be one of the centres of world attention.

(5) _____, there are some serious modifications to be made to your main grandstand and other facilities. (6) _____, the Press Committee insists that proper provision should be made for the hundreds of journalists who will be covering the matches. (7) _____, this will include telephones, typewriters, secretarial and translation services, as well as canteen facilities, but the Press Committee will contact you direct with details. (8) _____, this will require considerable expenditure on your part, but, (9) _____, it would be in your interest to comply in full with the Press Committee's requests so that all the reporters feel at home with you.

(10) _____, I am sure that I will be able to persuade the President of the committee to ratify the provisional acceptance provided you make it obvious that you are willing to cooperate, though, of course, I cannot say this openly.

Yours faithfully,

Peter Marks

P J W Marks (Secretary to the Arrangements Committee)

1 a) Evidently   b) Generally speaking   c) If I may say so
2 a) Obviously   b) Personally   c) Strictly speaking
3 a) technically   b) admittedly   c) personally
4 a) Naturally   b) Apparently   c) Frankly
5 a) Ideally   b) Unfortunately   c) In theory
6 a) Quite properly   b) Eventually   c) Presumably
7 a) To be honest   b) Presumably   c) Surely
8 a) In theory   b) Obviously   c) Eventually
9 a) admittedly   b) in my opinion   c) roughly speaking
10 a) In short   b) Confidentially   c) Apparently

2.5 FIRST AND LAST SENTENCES

The first and last sentences of the following letter are missing. Working in groups of two or three, choose the most appropriate suggestions from those given below the letter. Then compare your answers and your reasons with those of other groups.

```
Lost Property Office,
British Rail,
London SW1


Dear Sirs,

...........................................................

...........................................................
I had the wallet when I boarded the 8.30 London-Norwich train, and I
consulted something in it soon after the train left London, some-
where around Harlow.  I did not need it again until I wanted to pay
for a taxi in Norwich.  It was not in the taxi, and I therefore
conclude that I must have dropped it on the train during the part
of the journey from Harlow to Norwich.  The wallet is of brown
leather, and it contained several credit cards in my name, as well
as some £20 in cash.  I travelled in a second-class non-smoker in,
I think, the second carriage from the front.

...........................................................

...........................................................
Yours faithfully,

Lucy Warner

(Mrs. J. B. Warner)
```

Choices for first sentence:

a) My wallet, which I seem to have lost, was a present from my husband.
b) Some people keep money in a pocket, but I prefer to keep it in my good-quality wallet.
c) Have you got my wallet by any chance?
d) I am writing to you to ask about my wallet, which I lost yesterday.

Choices for last sentence:

a) Some time ago I lost my umbrella on a train, and on that occasion you were kind enough to return it to me.
b) I would be very grateful if you could let me know if it has been handed in to you.
c) If I found somebody else's wallet, I would most definitely hand it in to the stationmaster.
d) I am sure you find hundreds of wallets every day, but if you look carefully, you might find mine.

2.6 SELECTION AND ORDERING OF INFORMATION

A friend of yours is planning to study English at a language school in England. He or she is preparing a letter to the school asking for and giving information. He or she has made the following notes of possible things to include. Working in groups of two or three, decide which points to include and why you think the other points should not be included.

How many students are there in each class?
How many hours per week are the courses?
I live near the British Institute, and know some of the teachers there.
How long do the courses last?
I have been to England twice before.
Is the school far from the centre of London?
How much do the courses cost?
Is the school in a modern or an old building?
What is the total number of students in the school?
Is there a discotheque near the school?
Does the school have a language laboratory?
I like English very much.
Is the school a member of the Association of Registered English Language
    Schools?
Are the teachers old or young?
How many speakers of my language would there be in my class?
Is it a good school?
I have been studying English for 3 years, 3 hours a week, at the Royal School.
Would I have a lot of homework?
What is included in the cost of the courses? Travel? Books? Excursions?
    Accommodation?
My teacher says I speak English very well.

Now group together the points you have decided to include to form paragraphs. Finally, write the letter, using a suitable first and last sentence.

Follow-up activity

You have seen an advertisement in a newspaper in which an English family offers to take a foreign child into their home as a paying guest for a month. You are interested in sending your 12-year-old son or daughter to stay with this family. Write to the family giving and asking for information. Working in groups of four or five, spend ten minutes writing down as many ideas as you can for possible inclusion in the letter. Do not discuss the ideas at the same time. At the end of the 10-minute period, look at the list you have written, choose the most important ideas, group them into paragraphs, and then write the letter.

2.7 TEXT COMPARISON

The following are two applications for a British Council scholarship to study in Britain. Working in groups of two or three, decide which you prefer and why. Then discuss your decision and reasons with other groups. Finally, write a letter of application for a scholarship, based on the information at the end.

Dear Sirs,

    I would like to apply for a British Council Scholarship to study in Britain. I am in my final year of a 5-year degree course in civil engineering at Munich University. In our last two years we have to choose an optional subject, and I have opted for town planning, with special reference to city centres. My working experience is limited to four months, (July to September of last year and the year before,) as an unpaid assistant in the planning office of the Munich City Council.

    I am not involved in any current research, but my reading has included many articles and reports, several of which were from Great Britain and the USA, on traffic-free shopping centres. It is this particular aspect of town planning that interests me because the centres of many German towns suffer from the dense traffic there. The reason I would like to study in Britain is to have the opportunity of working with those planners who are responsible for present and future developments in this area.

    I understand that Leeds and Birmingham universities are heavily engaged in this work, and consequently, I hope that I would be able to do my post-graduate work in one of these. As for the period, at least one year would suit me, starting next autumn or at any time after that.

    I look forward to hearing from you.

                      Yours faithfully,

                      Hans Namberger.

                      J. C. Namberger.

Dear Sirs,

Britain is where things are happening in my particular field. I have very little experience, but my degree allows for the specialisation in the planning of town centres. As far as I can see, Leeds and Birmingham would be good places to study. At the end of this year my course will end, and I would like to go on studying

traffic-free centres. I have worked in the planning
office of Munich City Council, but only for four months.

Several of the reports which I have read, although not
exactly research, were produced in Great Britain and the
USA, and traffic is a big problem in the centre of many
German towns, too. If I could study, say, for one year,
then that would continue my optional subject. The period
could be any time starting next autumn, because my 5-year
degree course in civil engineering ends at Munich University
this summer.

I was not paid while I was working in July and September
in the planning office, but I would like to do post-
graduate work in the same field. I understand that Leeds
and Birmingham have experts in traffic-free shopping
centres, and I should like to apply for a British Council
Scholarship to study in Britain.

I look forward to hearing from you.

Rupert Haydn.

Name	Juan Lopez Gomez
Address	84 Calle Arrallo, Barcelona 15, Spain
Birth	31 March 1955; Salamanca, Spain
First degree	Doctor of Medicine, University of Salamanca, (1974-79)
Postgraduate study	One-year course in ophthalmology, University of Barcelona, (1979-80)
Special interest	Suitability of different types of contact lenses
Present post	Since 1980, contract at the Eye Clinic of Barcelona General Hospital; contract ends in one year.
Publications	Article 'Soft and Rigid Contact Lenses', published in <u>The Lancet</u>, 1980. Article based on survey of 37 patients over 6 months. This article led to correspondence with Dr Jermyn at St Thomas's Hospital, London and with Dr Askerholm at University College Hospital, London.
Current research	Adaptation and suitability of various types of contact lenses; 200 patients over 2 years.
	Require British Council scholarship for two years to study with Jermyn or Askerholm; period to begin at end of contract with Barcelona Eye Clinic.

2.8   TEXT BASED ON VISUAL INFORMATION

The factory behind Denver High School (see Fig. 1) applied for permission to build near Redd's Lane. Read the following letter, which rejects the application and gives the reasons for the refusal. Then, working in groups of two or three, study Fig. 2. You are going to write a letter of refusal in reply to an application for permission to build the Bossit Cross Hotel. Think of the different individuals or groups who might have objections to the proposal, and what their arguments might be. Finally, write the letter.

ARCHITECTS DEPARTMENT
DENVER TOWN COUNCIL
Denver DV1 1SB

Dear Sirs,

                    EXPANSION OF FACTORY PREMISES:

          Planning Permission Application No. PDR/4359/83

With reference to your application for permission to build additional factory premises in the area between Redd's Lane and Essex Road, adjoining Denver High School, I regret to inform you that, after careful consideration, the planning committee has decided to refuse permission on the following grounds.

   Firstly, the Local Education Authority has filed a provisional application for the use of this land as a school playing field for Denver High School, which at present does not have such a facility. It is almost certain, providing the necessary funds can be found, that this scheme will go ahead.

   Secondly, the Residents' Association of the Padgett Park Estate has frequently complained about the smoke and smell caused by your present installations, and consequently, they are hostile to any suggestion of further factory premises.

   Thirdly, as the Council transport committee has pointed out, there are no direct trunk road or rail links with your factory, and Redd's Lane is unsuited to the sort of traffic that serves your factory; it would obviously be even more unsuitable for an increase in such traffic.

   Fourthly and finally, the religious order at The Priory have claimed that a new factory building in Redd's Lane would be totally out of keeping with the architecture of The Priory itself and with similar buildings nearby.

May I, in conclusion, apologise on behalf of the committee for any inconvenience caused by the delay in reaching our decision.

Yours faithfully,

Basil Pride

B.R.W. Pride, MA, FRIArch,
Chief Architect

Redd's Lane
Denver DV5 4RT

23 June 1982

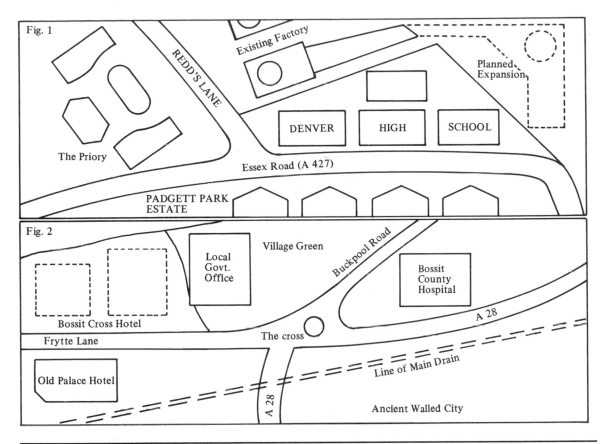

Fig. 1

Existing Factory

REDD'S LANE

Planned Expansion

DENVER   HIGH   SCHOOL

The Priory

Essex Road (A 427)

PADGETT PARK ESTATE

Fig. 2

Village Green

Local Govt. Office

Buckpool Road

Bossit County Hospital

A 28

Bossit Cross Hotel

Frytte Lane

The cross

A 28

Line of Main Drain

Old Palace Hotel

Ancient Walled City

2.9 IDEAS FOR LETTERS

Choose one of the following topics, or any other topic that interests you.

First, *write down in ten minutes as many ideas on the subject as you can.*

Then *look through all the ideas, and decide if there are some that are not particularly important or relevant, and can therefore be left out.*

After that, *group the ideas that you have, and decide on the best order, both within each group and among the groups.*

Now *compose each paragraph, linking the ideas together with suitable words and phrases.*

Finally, *bearing in mind the content of the whole letter, write a suitable introduction, and also a suitable conclusion.*

a) A letter of application for a job of your choice. (Compare 2.2.)
b) A letter replying to the one in 2.4, taking up each of the points, and assuring Mr Marks that everything he mentions – and more – will be provided.
c) A letter to the Lost Property Department of British Airways, enquiring about something you think you left on a plane. (Compare 2.5.)
d) A letter of application for a scholarship to do further studies in Britain in your own field. (Compare 2.7.)
e) A reply to the letter in 2.8, detailing how all the objections may be overcome, and appealing for the application to be reconsidered.

3 Formal letters II

3.1 PUNCTUATION

Working in groups of two or three, compare the following pairs of sentences, and decide whether (a) or (b) is correct. In some cases both (a) and (b) are possible, but with different meanings. What is the difference in meaning in these cases? Then compare your answers with those of other groups.

1   a) Everest which is the highest mountain in the world was not climbed until 1953.
    b) Everest, which is the highest mountain in the world, was not climbed until 1953.

2   a) The river that runs through Paris is called the Seine.
    b) The river that runs through Paris, is called the Seine.

3   a) They were sent some silk by their cousin who is in the merchant navy.
    b) They were sent some silk by their cousin, who is in the merchant navy.

4   a) We need someone who can read Chinese.
    b) We need someone, who can read Chinese.

5   a) Thank you for your letter which arrived today.
    b) Thank you for your letter, which arrived today.

6   a) Mr Branston who is a rather shy man does not like making speeches.
    b) Mr Branston, who is a rather shy man, does not like making speeches.

7   a) We got in through the window which somebody had left open.
    b) We got in through the window, which somebody had left open.

8   a) They accused my father who is scrupulously honest of fraud.
    b) They accused my father, who is scrupulously honest, of fraud.

9   a) Could you please let us know the dates, which would suit you best?
    b) Could you please let us know the dates which would suit you best?

10 a) The girls who worked hard were given a bonus.
    b) The girls, who worked hard, were given a bonus.

Now, working individually, punctuate the following sentences. If there are two possibilities, decide what the different meanings would be. Then compare your answers with those of others.

11 Winston Churchill who was unpopular with many people became Prime Minister.

12 We will have to return the parcel which was delivered today.

13 What is the name of the mountains which divide Spain from France?

14 The Pyrenees which divide Spain from France are often covered with snow.

15 The supplies which we kept in the shed rapidly became mouldy.

16 The young lady who served us last time now works in a different shop.

17 Politicians who are dishonest should be punished severely.

18 My brother interviewed all the people who had escaped unhurt.

19 The committee that is responsible includes her mother and father who are both lawyers.

20 The German car which won the race was driven by an Austrian.

3.2   SCRAMBLED SENTENCES

The following sentences go together to form a complete letter, but they are in the wrong order. Working in groups of two or three, put them in the right order, and decide how the words and phrases underlined help to link the text together. Then compare your answers with those of other groups.

Dear Sir,

a) I telephoned the council offices, but I was merely told that in the last six months no traffic lights had been installed anywhere, and that this was due to economy cuts.

b) However, nothing has been done.

c) It would be interesting if someone in authority could try to explain this strange - and dangerous - order of priorities.

d) This crossroads is an accident black spot.

e) Now, as you know, the need for these traffic lights has once again been tragically underlined by another death, this time of a young child.

f) I am writing to draw your readers' attention to the urgent need for traffic lights at the junction of Mars Road and Sale Street.

g) This reply is totally unsatisfactory when, as everyone knows, the council has recently spent enormous amounts of money on the installation of new public lavatories in Town Hall Square.

h) After a fatal accident some six months ago the council promised to install traffic lights there.

i) I do not normally make public protests, but this latest incident made me act.

j) It has been the scene of dozens of bad accidents, including several in which people have died.

Yours faithfully,

Brenda Bradey

(Mrs) J. B. Bradey.

3.3   LINKING WORDS AND PHRASES

In the following letter the linking words and phrases are missing. Working in groups of two or three, choose the most appropriate word or phrase from the ones given below. Then compare your answers with those of other groups.

Dear Sir,

I am writing to express my opinion about what you suggested in your article called 'Dole Giveaway', (1) .... that the Social Security system was being abused by people doing casual work while drawing benefit, and that (2) .... it should be reduced or (3) .... abolished.

(4) ...., let me say that I am the unemployed head of a family of six, and that all my four children are at school, (5) .... I am entitled to draw only the minimum benefits. (6) ...., we are always short of money. (7) ...., unemployment is running at 15% in this area, so there is little chance of finding a job, at least not at my age (54). I (8) .... feel that I am entitled to full support from the state. (9) ...., when I was working, I paid taxes, like everybody else. ((10) ...., I still have to pay Value Added Tax even now!)

(11) ...., many people that I know are out of work, though most of them would prefer to be working. None of them have any money to spare, but (12) .... I know of only one man who abuses the system. (13) ...., I know of many who, for some reason or another, do not draw their full entitlement.

(14) ...., I would like to ask if the author of the article has ever been out of work himself. (15) ...., I think that he had better keep his opinions to himself until he knows what he is talking about. There are far too many people who get away with writing about things that they really know nothing about.

Yours faithfully,

Adam Smithson.

Adam Smithson

1   a) for example   b) namely   c) therefore   d) in other words
2   a) thus   b) for this reason   c) so   d) on the other hand
3   a) what's more   b) at any rate   c) even   d) at last
4   a) In the first place   b) Next   c) Furthermore   d) In fact
5   a) yet   b) though   c) however   d) because
6   a) By comparison   b) In spite of that   c) As a result   d) All the same
7   a) However   b) For instance   c) What is more   d) On the other hand

8 a) therefore   b) by comparison   c) for example   d) because
9 a) Otherwise   b) After all   c) Equally   d) By the way
10 a) At any rate   b) That is to say   c) In other words   d) Incidentally
11 a) Alternatively   b) Even   c) Secondly   d) On the other hand
12 a) Even   b) In spite of that   c) By the way   d) Although
13 a) In that case   b) Alternatively   c) For example   d) On the contrary
14 a) To sum up   b) Finally   c) Therefore   d) In the end
15 a) In that case   b) If so   c) Therefore   d) If not

Each of the following examples has a blank where there should be a linking word or phrase. Working individually, choose from the words above one that clearly brings out the relationship between the two statements. Try not to use the same answer twice. Then compare your answers with those of others.

16 My grandmother has been blind for many years. .... she insists on living alone and doing everything for herself.
17 Your article stated that teachers' salaries were low, and that they should .... be given a substantial rise.
18 I would like to know if your correspondent has visited many state schools. ...., his opinions about them are worthless.
19 I agree entirely with your suggestion for our city centre, ... that it should become a traffic-free zone.
20 My husband and I are not satisfied with the Council's way of dealing with ratepayers' complaints. ...., they are supposed to be our servants, not we theirs.
21 The children round here often do errands for the neighbours. ...., they often help people in other parts of the town.
22 I have to do two jobs to support my family. .... I have very little spare time.
23 My 8-year-old son often cooks dinner for the family. On occasions he has .... cooked a meal for visitors.

3.4 ATTITUDE WORDS AND PHRASES

The blanks in the following letter must be filled with words and phrases that bring out the writer's attitude to what he is saying. Working in groups of two or three, choose the most appropriate suggestion from the ones given below. Then compare your answers with those of other groups.

Dear Sir,

    I am writing concerning last week's editorial, 'Discipline in our Schools'. (1) ...., I do not write letters to newspapers, but I feel that I have to write on this occasion. (2) ...., I got extremely angry when I read the editorial, which virtually maintained that discipline is the same as cruelty.

    (3) ...., when I was at school, we were told what to do, and we did it. (4) ...., if we did not, we were punished. And if we repeatedly refused to obey, we were punished severely. (5) ...., this may seem hard to some people, and (6) ...., we resented it at the time. But we did not really suffer, and we learnt certain values and a certain self-respect.

    (7) ...., I am convinced that discipline is essential if children are to have a sense of security. (8) ...., a child needs to know what is right and what is wrong, i.e. it needs moral guidance. (9) ...., to judge from their behaviour in public, many children nowadays have no such guidance. (10) ...., physical cruelty would be going too far, but good sound discipline would make these young people happier with themselves and better members of society.

                    Yours faithfully,

                    (Major) Jarvis Pritchart.

---

1   a) Generally speaking   b) Of course   c) Personally
2   a) Frankly   b) Literally   c) In my opinion
3   a) Strictly   b) Personally   c) Quite properly
4   a) In short   b) Naturally   c) Undoubtedly
5   a) As a matter of fact   b) Of course   c) Indeed
6   a) evidently   b) in brief   c) understandably
7   a) Personally   b) Apparently   c) To be precise
8   a) With respect   b) Obviously   c) Technically
9   a) Clearly   b) Practically   c) Unjustly
10   a) Really   b) Officially   c) Admittedly

3.5 REPORTING WORDS

There are two reported speech versions of the following direct speech. Working in groups of two or three, decide which you prefer and why. In particular, consider the role of the reporting word claim. *Then discuss your conclusion with other groups.*

'There's no doubt about it, madam,' said the store manager. 'We never make mistakes.'

a) The store manager told me that there was no doubt about it. They never made mistakes.
b) The store manager claimed that they never made mistakes.

Now report the following items of direct speech, choosing in each case one of the reporting words given. Then compare your answers with those of others.

accuse; wonder; offer; deny; doubt; mean; refuse; announce; complain; apologise.

1 'What will happen if I refuse?' Jim said quietly to himself.
2 'I'm afraid that the Council cannot treat your case as urgent,' the letter said.
3 'There's no point in trying to deny it, Sheila,' her boyfriend said. 'You've been going out with other men behind my back.'
4 'Don't start suggesting that I was responsible,' Fred said. 'I wasn't even here when the fire started.'
5 'Ladies and gentlemen, the flight will leave at about 3 o'clock,' said the official.

Now choose two or three of the reporting words that you have not so far used; write examples of direct speech and reported speech to illustrate the use of these words.

3.6 FIRST AND LAST SENTENCES

The first and last sentences of the following letter are missing. Working in groups of two or three, choose the most appropriate suggestions from those given below the letter. Decide what makes a good first sentence and a good last sentence. Then compare your answers with those of other groups.

Dear Sir,

    ....

There are several reasons why I object to these places. Firstly, the owners take quite substantial amounts of money away from the people who are least able to afford it, namely the old, under the false promise of an easy fortune. Secondly, while I do not object to gambling in principle, I feel that this particular kind, where no skill is required on the part of the player, is especially offensive and deadening to the intellect. Thirdly, these establishments often attract undesirable individuals into the neighbourhood. Lastly, the physical appearance of these places, with their gaudy neon lights and their coloured plastic hoardings, is totally out of keeping with the quiet restful appearance of our town.

In conclusion, let me say that I do not wish to appear old-fashioned or anti-pleasure. ....

Yours faithfully,

Freda Cunningham

(Miss) Freda Cunningham.

Choices for first sentence:

a) In the last eight years over 2,000 bingo halls have opened in Britain.
b) I have played bingo only once, and as a matter of fact I won fifty pounds.
c) I live alone in a bungalow opposite a bingo hall.
d) Old people need special recreation centres, not bingo halls.
e) I would like to express my concern at the growing number of bingo halls in our town.

Choices for last sentence:

a) Of course, some old people – especially bingo 'regulars' – like the atmosphere, the neon lights and – occasionally – the winnings.
b) I am in favour of betting on horses and, though with certain reservations, football pools because these do require a certain element of skill on part of the punter.
c) However, I hope that the Council, who grant the licences for these places, will consider very carefully whether this mindless kind of entertainment is what is wanted in this traditionally peaceful town.
d) There are many other things that worry me about this town as well as bingo, especially the heavy drinking that goes on, and also the number of dirty books that you can buy anywhere.
e) When I say 'undesirable individuals', I do not mean the people of this town, but rather the hordes of young louts who come down from London on their motorbikes.

Now, working in groups of two or three, work out what the main purpose of the following letter is, and write a suitable first sentence and last sentence for it.

Dear Sir,

....

....

There are several reasons why I object to these places. Firstly,
the people who run them take a lot of money away from young
people in exchange for a certain relief from their boredom.
Secondly, although I do not object to young boys and girls having
fun, I feel that most of the machines are fixed so that you can
very rarely win. Thirdly, I feel that it would be much better
for these young people to be doing something in the open air
instead of in a smoky atmosphere. I am sure they would enjoy
it more, too. Lastly, the physical appearance of these places is
most unattractive, and there is almost always a lot of noise
around them, which is not at all in keeping with the traditionally
quiet atmosphere of our little village........................

....

....

Yours faithfully,

Gilbert Hoskins

Gilbert Hoskins.

3.7 SELECTION AND ORDERING OF INFORMATION

You are going to write a letter to a local newspaper appealing for support for a project to help old people in your area. You have collected the following points, but they are not all equally important. In any case, newspapers prefer short letters. Working in groups of two or three, decide which of the points are important enough to be included, and then group them into paragraphs. Then plan each paragraph carefully, and finally write the letter.

There are at least 5,000 people over the age of 65 in your town.
Not many old people play tennis.
There's a bingo hall and four cinemas in your town.
Cinemas are cheap for old age pensioners (OAPs) in the morning.
The state pension is only 25 pounds a week.
Your uncle is 78 years old.
OAPs need a recreation centre.
OAPs need food and heat.

Many old people can't move around a lot.

Old people are often bad-tempered because their memory fails.

You are going to organise a voluntary visiting service for old people.

You need volunteers to help in your various projects.

You know a lot of old people.

You are going to organise a scheme to help old people decorate their houses.

Old people drive very slowly.

Your group now has 25 volunteer members.

Some old people have cars.

You have organised an emergency telephone service, which is manned all day.

The local government authority does very little for OAPs.

Brain cells do not regenerate, and this is one reason why old people lose their sight.

The local 'Meals-on Wheels' service produces 369 meals per day.

There are many OAPs in your street.

People's reaction time slows down considerably when they get older.

Many old people fought in the war.

You need money to help with your expenses, especially the emergency phone.

You visit the hospital every week.

The Rev. Harris goes with you to the hospital.

Old people are difficult to get on with, and therefore often lonely.

Old people get on well with children, and tell them stories.

Donations can be sent to Hutchins Bank, High Street, account no. WL 25667.

You started your action group by talking to friends.

The first meeting of the group will be in the Black Bull at 8 p.m. on Friday, 28 October.

You have plans to build a community centre for OAPs if you can get enough money.

The government sometimes gives OAPs a substantial rise.

Many old people need special attention, and this requires a lot of patience and tolerance on the part of the volunteer helper.

Follow-up activity

You are going to write a letter to a local newspaper appealing for support for a project to help young people in your town, and to provide a youth club for poor children who otherwise would have nowhere to go in the evenings*. Working in groups of four or five, spend ten minutes writing down as many ideas as you can think of for possible inclusion in the letter. Do not discuss the ideas at the same time. At the end of the 10-minute period, look at the list you have written, choose the most important ideas, group them into paragraphs, and then write the letter.

* or if you prefer, you can choose one of these suggestions:
   The Royal National Lifeboat Institution
   The Royal National Institute for the Blind
   Oxfam (an organisation which provides food, clothing, medicine, etc. for people in the Third World)
   The Salvation Army
   The Campaign for the Legalisation of Marijuana

3.8 TEXT COMPARISON

Working in groups of two or three, decide which of the following letters you prefer, and why. Then discuss your decision with other groups. Finally, rewrite the letter you did not like.

Dear Sir,

Last Sunday a friend of mine and I were spending a pleasant afternoon in the garden, when some workmen started making a terrible noise in the street outside. I went to ask them what was going on, and they explained that they were digging up the road to repair the gas pipes. I fully understand that the gas company cannot send workmen only at times convenient to me, but I feel very strongly that Sunday is the wrong day to choose. Do we, the citizens of Bradfield, have to accept anything that these so-called service companies choose to do?

Yours faithfully,

Tina Brockhouse

(Miss) T. F. Brockhouse

Dear Sir,

Last Saturday we were spending a pleasant afternoon playing bridge on the large balcony, when they started making an awful noise in the road. I went to ask them what was happening, and they told me that they were digging it up to repair them. The man said that he understood my complaint, and would pass it on to them. I fully realise that the water company cannot send them only at times which suit me, but in my opinion it seems to be the wrong day to choose. Must we always accept what they decide to do?

Yours faithfully,

James Thwaite

J. E. Thwaite.

3.9 TEXT BASED ON VISUAL INFORMATION

The local newspaper in your town has offered a thousand pounds for the best design of a new Sports and Recreation Centre (SRC). The letter and Fig. 1 are one entry. Look at the design, and read the letter explaining how and why the design was planned. Then either write an explanatory letter to accompany Fig. 2, or design your own SRC and write an explanatory letter to accompany your design.

Dear Sir,

      I enclose our entry for the Linton Gazette SRC design competition. It was designed by my brother Jerry and me, and we have tried to provide something for everybody, whatever their interests. The design is largely self-explanatory, but here are some of the reasons behind our ideas.

1. <u>Sports</u> – Although there are already several football pitches in the area, we have included a full-size one, because football is the most popular sport. The pitch can, of course, also be used for hockey and other sports. Tennis is another popular sport, and we have included three hard courts which, if they are well looked after, could be used all year round. As regards swimming, since there is a large municipal baths nearby, we did not think a full-size pool was necessary, but we have included a small open-air pool for summer use.

2. <u>Facilities</u> – We have situated the changing rooms between the two areas of sports activities so that they are easily accessible, whatever the sport. Adjoining the changing rooms we have planned a simple cinema, which could easily be converted into a theatre, concert hall, meeting hall or dance hall. We haven't included a nursery because we feel that it is unlikely that both parents, even if they bring their children, will want to play something at the same time.

3. <u>Car parks</u> – We have included separate car-parking space as near as possible to each area of activity to avoid congestion. At times of need, the sports pitch car park can obviously supplement the cinema car park, and vice versa.

4. <u>General</u> – We think the place should look attractive, not least because one form of leisure activity, particularly for the old, is walking around pleasant gardens and among trees. We envisage one-storey buildings throughout, and as large an area as possible should be covered with trees and shrubs.

To sum up, we have tried to think of the centre as a facility to be enjoyed by all members of the community. We have taken account of the need to provide car parks, but we have not overlooked the need to keep the overall design both attractive and simple. We also hope that the cost of our plan, if adopted, would be relatively low.

     Yours faithfully,

     Marion Ratcliff

     Marion Ratcliff (also for Jerry Ratcliff)

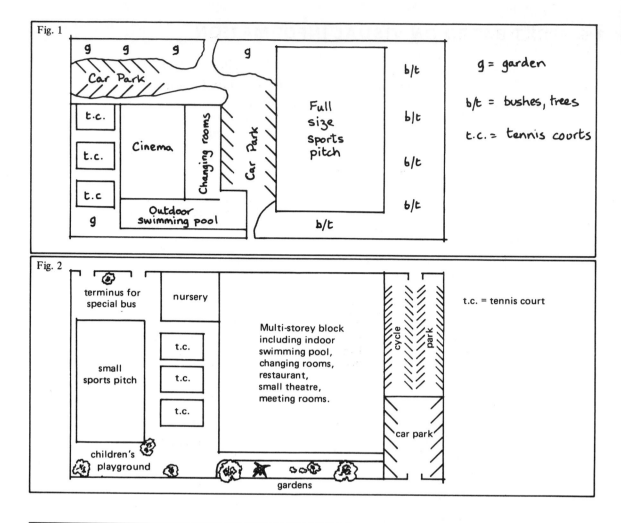

Fig. 1

g   g   g   g

Car Park

b/t   b/t   b/t   b/t

Full size sports pitch

t.c.   t.c.   t.c.

Cinema

Changing rooms

Car Park

g   Outdoor swimming pool   b/t

g = garden

b/t = bushes, trees

t.c. = tennis courts

Fig. 2

terminus for special bus   nursery

t.c. = tennis court

small sports pitch

t.c.   t.c.   t.c.

Multi-storey block including indoor swimming pool, changing rooms, restaurant, small theatre, meeting rooms.

cycle   park

car park

children's playground

gardens

3.10 LETTER ON A THEME

The following news article, editorial and letter all appeared in the same local newspaper on the same day; they all refer to the controversy concerning Bartlett Street. The letter from Councillor Hawkesworth is incomplete; working in groups of three or four complete the letter by going through the following steps:

1 *Spend ten minutes simply thinking of possible ideas and noting them down.*
2 *Choose the most important ideas.*
3 *Decide on a suitable order for your ideas.*
4 *Decide how many paragraphs the letter will need.*
5 *Write the letter using linking words (because, however, first, second, etc.) to make clear the relations between the ideas.*

Then compare your letter with those of other groups.

Finally, work individually to write David Hanson's letter, which is NOT *a reply to Hawkesworth, but simply states Hanson's point of view. Compare your letter with those of other students.*

Bartlett Street Barricades

The inhabitants of Bartlett Street, in response to the private initiative of 28-year-old school-master David Henson, have acted to do something about the condition of their neighbour-hood. They have collectively painted the fronts of all the houses in the street, cleared away all the rubbish, repaired all the fittings, and helped some of the older residents to paint the inside of their houses.

What's more they have written to the local authority proposing that bollards be erected at each end of the street, so that no cars can enter. They then intend to set up an adventure playground running practically the whole length of the street. 'If they don't agree, we'll put up our own barricades,' said Henson last night.

Hawkesworth hostile

Councillor James Hawkesworth (54) was 'bitterly opposed' to any such scheme. 'Leave our streets alone,' he said at an emergency meeting of the cor-poration late last night. He claimed that the streets were part of the town, and as such did not belong to the people who happened to live there. Henson and his student 'friends' had no right at all to bring the traffic to a standstill so that a 'handful of kids could play at cowboys and indians'.

Hawkesworth then went on to point out that there were a num-ber of purely practical reasons why the scheme was unwork-able. According to him emerg-ency services wouldn't be able to get through to certain parts of the town, traffic congestion would be much worse in the town centre at certain hours, and even the inhabitants of Bart-lett Street would suffer in the long run.

The councillor finished an ex-tremely hostile speech by ques-tioning Henson's motives, and by drawing particular attention to Henson's barricade statement, which, he said, was evidence of 'sheer irresponsibility'. The corporation, in spite of Hawkes-worth's protests, agreed to defer decision until they had made a thorough examination of Hen-son's proposals.

Comment

Bartlett Street Controversy

The Bartlett Street controv-ersy has reached dangerous proportions, and surely now is the time to take a cold, hard look at the facts be-fore somebody gets hurt. An apparently well-meaning in-dividual has decided to take action on behalf of his neighbours, and he has come up against administrative opposition.

Perhaps if he had been more tactful in the present-ation of his case, he might have had a more sympa-thetic hearing. On the other hand, if the corporation had been more interested in the conditions in Bartlett Street, none of this would have been necessary. On this page we have printed letters from Mr Henson and from Cllr Hawkesworth. Let us hope that both parties will con-sider the argument care-fully, from both points of view, and realise that neither has a monopoly of the truth.

Letters

From Cllr J Hawkesworth

Dear Sir,
May I use your columns to appeal to the citizens of this town to return to common sense. Although Mr Henson has perhaps done us the ser-vice of drawing our attention to the conditions in Bartlett Street, there are several rea-sons why we must reject his plan.   *(cont. on page 4)*

3.11   IDEAS FOR LETTERS

Choose one of the following topics, or any other topic that interests you.
  First, *write down in ten minutes as many ideas on the subject as you can.*
  Then *look through all the ideas and decide if there are some that are not particularly important or relevant, and can therefore be left out.*
  After that, *group the ideas that you have, and decide on the best order, both within each group and among the groups.*
  Now, *compose each paragraph, linking the ideas together with suitable words and phrases.*
  Finally, *bearing in mind the content of the whole letter, write a suitable introduction, and also a suitable conclusion.*

a) A letter complaining about the inefficient bus service which you use every day to get to work. Explain the inconveniences that you and others have to put up with, and suggest ways of improving the service.
b) A letter asking for advice on how to learn a foreign language. Mention some of the ways that you have heard about or have tried, and ask readers to write in with their experiences.
c) A letter explaining about the treatment – good or bad – that you recently received during a visit to a foreign country or to another part of your own country.
d) A letter relating how you bought something, and later had to take it back to the shop three times before it would work properly.
e) A letter complaining about smoking in public places. Give as many reasons as possible against it, and suggest remedies.
f) A letter replying to Jarvis Pritchart's letter. (See 3.4.)
g) A letter announcing a forthcoming meeting, rally, exhibition, etc., of an amateur club or society of which you are one of the leaders.
h) A letter reporting a meeting you had with a local person who has recently done something difficult or interesting.

4 Reports

4.1 PUNCTUATION

Notice the lack of punctuation in the following sentences:

1   Mary said that she would never do it.
2   The woman over there is my teacher.
3   It is obvious that we ought to leave early.
4   When I wake depends on the time of the year.
5   She asked me if I was English.
6   They wanted to know where we were going.
7   How you do it is not very important.
8   A girl called Desdemona phoned while you were out.
9   I went to the shops to buy some fruit.
10 It is unwise to decide too quickly.
11 We'll go when you're ready.
12 They're so heavy I can't even move them on my own.

Now punctuate the following sentences:

13 They asked me if I knew him after they'd explained what he'd done.

14 A man dressed all in black walked up to her and bowed.

15 What you do in your own home is not my affair.

16 Jenny said that the work was very difficult It's not really difficult I said but it is time-consuming.

17 Her mother claimed that she was so clever she didn't need to study to pass her exams.

18 Fred said that it was important not to make too many mistakes.

19 Phone me if they arrive before I do.

20 It is fairly certain that they'll put the prices up again.

21 My sister is that girl reading the newspaper and the one next to her is my cousin.

22 They wrote to us to find out what had caused the delay but we couldn't tell them anything.

23 They wanted to know whether I could start at once. Not at once I replied but perhaps by tomorrow afternoon.

24 I asked Jim if he could find the time to help me.

4.2 SCRAMBLED SENTENCES

The following sentences go together to form a newspaper report, but they are in the wrong order. Working in groups of two or three, put them in the right order, and decide how the words and phrases in bold type help to link the text together. Then compare your answers with those of other groups.

Ship accident in Channel

No Casualties

a) **In spite of this damage** the two ships managed to reach the nearby port of Dunkirk under their own steam.

b) **However,** because of the weather conditions, the captains did not realise the danger until only seconds before the collision took place.

c) **One** was a cargo boat carrying fruit, and apparently bound for London.

d) **The official added** that British experts would be invited to join **the committee.**

e) Fortunately, there were no casualties among the crews or the passengers, but both ships were holed close to the water-line.

f) According to eye-witnesses **neither of the vessels** was going very fast at the time of the accident.

g) Yesterday evening two ships collided in thick fog in the English Channel.

h) **Consequently,** there was insufficient time for them to take avoiding action.

i) **The other** was a British Rail cross-channel ferry on its regular run from Dover to Dunkirk.

j) A spokesman for **the port authorities** said that a committee of enquiry would be set up to ascertain the cause of the collision.

4.3   LINKING WORDS AND PHRASES

*Working in groups of two or three, complete the following three passages using
the words and phrases given. Then discuss your answers with other groups.*

A   I don't know whether you heard that I was a member of the club team in the
folk dancing competition last month. (1) ....At first........, I didn't
think I was good enough, but we've danced several times in public recently, and
the leader said that I did very well, so (2) ....in the end........, I allowed
myself to be persuaded. When all the teams had danced, the jury took ages to
make up their minds, and we were so nervous we could hardly wait. But then the
foreman of the jury came onto the stage. '(3) ....(c) at last....!' I
whispered to my neighbour. We didn't win, but we were very glad to come
second.

1 a) First   b) Firstly   c) At first   d) At the beginning
2 a) in the end   b) at the end   c) lastly
3 a) In the end   b) At the end   c) At last   d) Lastly

B   Before we moved into our new flat, there were several things that we had to
arrange. (4) ....First........, we had to have a big wardrobe built in
the main bedroom. (5) ....Second........, we had to fit safer, stronger
locks to all the doors. We also had to have central heating installed because the
winters here can be very cold. And (6) ....lastly........, we had to get
the telephone connected because, as you know, I can't possibly manage in my
business without it.

4 a) At first   b) In the beginning   c) First   d) At the beginning
5 a) On the other hand   b) After   c) Second
6 a) in the end   b) at last   c) lastly   d) at the end

C   Let me give you a rough idea of what happens in the film.
(7) ....At the beginning of.... the film we meet a young man who is obviously
unhappy, and who clearly has no idea how to overcome his unhappiness. We
follow the man through various experiences which gradually change his picture
of himself, although (8) ....at first.... they do not make him
happier. But (9) ....at last...., as you might expect, he meets a
young girl, and he falls in love with her. This changes his life completely, and he
starts seeing the brighter side of things. Unfortunately, I can't tell you what
happens right (10) ....at the end.... because I fell asleep before it
finished.

7   a) In the beginning of   b) First in   c) At the beginning of
    d) At first in
8   a) firstly   b) at the beginning   c) at first
9   a) at the end   b) lastly   c) at last
10 a) in the end   b) at last   c) finally   d) at the end

implied - indirectly

Now, working in groups, work out the uses of the following three groups of words and phrases:

at first, at last, in the beginning, in the end;
first, firstly, last, lastly, finally;
at the beginning, at the end.

Now working individually, put a suitable expression in each of the blanks in the following passage:

I recently read a book about a young woman. (11) _at the beginning_ of the story she is living at home with her parents; she has a boring job, but she hopes for better things. One day she sees an advert for air hostesses. (12) _at first_ she doesn't know what to do, but then she talks to her friends, and they all think she should try for it. So (13) _in the end_ she decides to apply. She has to wait quite a long time for a reply, but then one day it arrives. '(14) _at last_!' she says. 'I thought it would never come.' The letter says that there are three conditions: (15) _first_, she must be over 21; second, she must be at least 165 centimetres tall; and (16) _last_, she must speak one foreign language well. It turns out that she does in fact fulfil all three conditions, so she writes again, and they reply asking her to come for an interview. Anyway, to cut a long story short, she gets the job, and right (17) _at the end_ she wins a competition for the Best Air Hostess of the Year.

4.4 FIRST PARAGRAPH

There are three suggestions for the first paragraph of the report that follows. Working in groups of two or three, decide which is the most appropriate, and why. Then compare your answer with those of other groups.

FEASIBILITY OF FLEXIBLE WORKING HOURS

a) We on the committee have spent a lot of time and effort on the question of hours. I mean, different people have different opinions, obviously, and it doesn't matter whether you ask people here or outside, they all have their own opinions about whether it's a good idea or not. And since you get so many different opinions, it's not easy for a committee to come to a final decision, but we have done what we think is right, and we hope that if anybody is not completely happy, they won't take our ideas personally.

b) Since 1976 everybody in this firm has worked 40 hours per week - previous to that the total was 44 hours for some people and 42½ for others - and we have no intention of changing the total. In any case, a change in the total number of hours would only be possible after proper negotiations between management and union representatives, and this is not the place to anticipate any such negotiations in the near or distant future.

c) This report concerns the feasibility of allowing members of staff to start and stop work at the times that suit them best; the obvious proviso is, of course, that everyone should still work a total of 40 hours per week, as we do now. The suggestion of flexible working hours was put forward to the directors by certain members of staff, particularly those who have young children at school.

The Personnel Officer was asked to look into the question, and his study had two aspects. First, he looked at the experience of other firms; he managed to contact four firms of similar size to ours, all of which have, or have tried, some variation of staff hours. While most of their comments were favourable, all of them had noted certain minor drawbacks. Some of these problems were connected with factors that are irrelevant to our particular case.

The second part of the investigation was to look carefully at our own working arrangements. Here, as you know, we began by asking everybody to predict the hours they would probably choose to work. This information was then circulated to all heads of department for comment, in particular with regard to potential problems and their solution.

All this experience and information was then studied by a committee which included a representative from every department. The committee was unanimous in its view that the advantages of flexible working hours in firms like ours will almost certainly outweigh the disadvantages. We have therefore decided on a trial period of 3 months, starting 1 April; at the end of that period the committee will take a final decision. Full details will be circulated to all staff in about one week's time.

4.5 SELECTION AND ORDERING OF INFORMATION

A young couple that you know, Mr and Mrs Stevens, have applied to adopt a baby. The adoption committee has asked you to write a confidential report to help the committee in its decision. You have jotted down the following points. Working in groups of two or three, decide which points are important enough to include; group the points; and link them together. Then decide if the letter needs an introductory and a concluding paragraph. If so, what should they say? Finally, write out the complete letter.

They are legally married; I went to their wedding.

She is an intelligent, well-educated woman.

She could have a better job, but she isn't very ambitious; she works as a typist for a businessman.

He is rather quiet and seems to find it difficult to talk to people.

He likes football a lot, but she doesn't, and they often argue about whether he should go to a match or not.

He has a fairly good job as a foreman in a factory that makes spare parts for cars.

She is 27 years old, but she says she's 22; he is 24.

She likes going to dances and meeting new people; sometimes she goes dancing on her own.

My next-door neighbour is a distant cousin of theirs and also knows them quite well.

Their flat is old and small, but they have a new family saloon car and a colour television.

An old aunt of his will probably leave him quite a lot of money when she dies.

They have several nieces and nephews; they seem to be fonder of the girls than the boys.

They don't dress very neatly, and they haven't got a modern washing machine.

They both love animals.

She goes to evening classes for drawing, and some of the pictures on their walls are by her.

They got married quickly because she thought – or at least she said she thought – she was pregnant.

He says he's a communist, but I don't think he's a member of the party.

They're not very interested in food; they eat mostly things like fish and chips, chicken and chips, and so on.

Her parents are middle class, and they don't particularly like their son-in-law, who is from a working-class background.

She sometimes goes to church, but I don't think she believes in it very much; I don't think they would christen their children if they had any.

They both say that they would very much like to adopt a child, but only one.

Their relatives often come to see them, and their nieces and nephews seem to enjoy the visits.

When he was 18, he won a medal for bravery for saving a young girl from drowning.

They seem to quarrel quite a lot, but I think that they are genuinely in love.

She makes a lot of her own clothes. Their flat is clean, but not very tidy.

4.6   TEXT COMPARISON

*The following are two suggestions for the first paragraph of a report on
breastfeeding which is intended to encourage mothers to breastfeed their babies.
Working in groups of two or three, decide which you prefer, and why, Then
discuss your decision with other groups.*

A   There are various reasons why breastfeeding – as even the manufacturers of
baby foods admit – is best for mother and baby. In the first place, the milk
comes ready-mixed, germ-free, and at the right temperature. Secondly, the
supply is portable, readily available and inexpensive. And finally, the quality
and quantity of the milk adjust automatically to the baby's needs, as long as the
mother eats and sleeps well and cultivates a quiet mind. Moreover, both mother
and baby derive great satisfaction from this shared pleasure, and it also builds
up the baby's defences against disease. Let us look at each of these points in
some detail.

B   There are various reasons why breastfeeding is best for mother and
baby – as even the manufacturers of baby foods admit. First, there are the
all-important health factors: breast milk is germ-free, and moreover, it builds up
the baby's defences against disease. Then there is the question of convenience,
since breast milk is available when and where you want it, is ready-mixed, and
comes at the right temperature. Thirdly, there is the cost: while mother may
have to eat a little more, she obviously does not have to buy bottles, sterilizing
equipment or packets of manufactured milk. Last but not least, there is the
psychological side, for both mother and baby derive great emotional satisfaction
from this shared pleasure. Let us look at each of these points in some detail.

*Now, working individually, write the first paragraph of a report which is
intended to encourage people to cycle more.*

4.7   TEXT BASED ON A CONVERSATION

*In Great Britain the Guide Dog Association provides some 300 dogs a year for
blind people, enabling them to get out of their homes and to move about more
freely. Each owner is expected to send a report at certain intervals, detailing his
or her experiences. Here is a conversation between a blind person and a friend
who is going to write a report to the Association for her to sign.*

A: Well, shall we get down to what you want to go into the report, Mary?
M: Yes, good idea. I'm supposed to send my first report after about a month,
     and tomorrow it will in fact be thirty days since I came home with Sheila.
A: Right. And what's the report supposed to say?
M: Well, obviously, they want to know the changes the dog has made in your
     life. For instance, in my case, I can now do for myself a lot of things that I
     couldn't do before.
A: Like what?

M: Well, as you know, you or my sister used to come and take me to work each morning, and someone from work used to bring me home in the afternoon. Now I can do all that on my own. Or rather, Sheila does it for me.

A: What else?

M: Well, of course, shopping is a lot easier now, and I feel a lot safer, too, especially on Saturday mornings when there's so much traffic about.

A: Does Sheila carry your shopping basket?

M: Oh, no, she has to keep all her concentration for the traffic and the other pedestrians. Anyway, apart from shopping, I've been out to do other things. I've been to the cinema once with you, haven't I? But you didn't have to come and fetch me this time. And another time with my mother to see, oh I can't remember now what it was called. And another time when I just went on my own. It was that film about Eva Peron. They'd said it was good at work, so I just went.

A: You didn't tell me about that.

M: No, that's the point, you see. I can just go without having to trouble anyone else.

A: It's no trouble, Mary. You know that.

M: No, I know, but it's different not to have to rely on someone to help you. You feel more independent. Anyway, I've also been to two concerts. One with the London Symphony Orchestra, I think it was, and the other was a folk music evening, mostly singers from South America.

A: O.K. Any other differences?

M: Yes. I get to talk to people more than before. As you know, apart from her work looking after me, Sheila also has to go out and play. So I always go to the park in the evening and let her have a good long run. She really enjoys that.

A: Yes, but you were saying something about meeting people.

M: Yes, exactly. You see, when I went everywhere with my sister or with you, I talked to you but I never started talking to other people. Now I get out more often anyway, and since I'm not with anyone except Sheila, people are more likely to come up and ask me if I need a hand. Of course, with Sheila at my side, the answer is usually 'no', but we get talking. That's why I mentioned taking Sheila for a walk in the park. You see, there are always several other dog owners who take their dogs for a walk at the same time, and I've got quite friendly with several people that way.

A: And do you want to put anything about drawbacks? It can't all have been positive, can it?

M: Well, one thing that worries me is whether I'm giving Sheila enough food. I've never had a dog before, and perhaps we ought to ask how I can be sure she's eating enough. I'm sure they must have told me, but I've forgotten.

A: O.K. I'll ask.

M: The only other thing is, well, silly perhaps, but I'd like to mention it. It's that Sheila, you know, avoids all dangers, like cars and holes in the road, and so on. But she doesn't avoid puddles! So every time it rains I get my feet soaking wet because she doesn't bother to walk round any water there is about.

A: But otherwise no complaints.

M: No, none at all. Only thanks. Now I get more exercise because, as I said, I have to take Sheila out for a walk. And, then, with meeting new people and everything I feel a lot happier. You know that I sometimes used to get quite depressed, sitting here on my own night after night. Now I can go out and cheer myself up, and even if I stay at home, I don't feel alone because Sheila keeps me company.

Now, working in groups of two or three, prepare and write the report in the form of a letter to the Guide Dog Association. First, read through the conversation again, and underline the points that are important enough to include in the report. Then group the points together, and write a separate paragraph for each group of points. Finally, write a suitable introductory paragraph and a suitable concluding paragraph to complete the report.

4.8 TEXT BASED ON VISUAL INFORMATION

Read the report below in conjunction with the diagram at the side of it.

DRILLING CONDITIONS IN UJIKSHTAN

The first two or three feet were relatively easy to drill through, but after passing through a layer of chalk, we came up against our first layer of hard basalt. At this stage we had to change the drilling head, and as a result the drilling became slower. As we carried on through this hard layer, we had to stop frequently to make sure that the bit was not overheating.

The third stage of our progress towards the oil was varied. There were sometimes hard rocks or pebbles, and sometimes soft chalk. Although the ground was softer on average than the second layer, we could not go much faster because it was never soft for long, and changing the bits is very time-consuming.

During the last stage we had to pass through even harder rock, and on many occasions the drilling bit did in fact overheat. However, through patience, and with some skilful work by the mechanics, we finally reached the oil deposits a week after we started drilling.

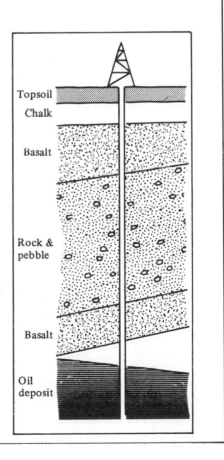

Topsoil
Chalk
Basalt
Rock & pebble
Basalt
Oil deposit

Now, working in groups of two or three, write an account of a journey you made by car from Lake Zurich to Lake Como last summer, basing your account on the diagrams below.

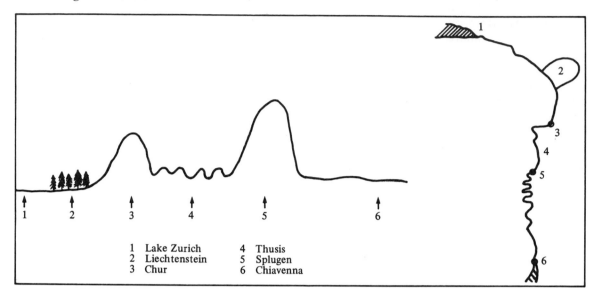

1 Lake Zurich	4 Thusis
2 Liechtenstein	5 Splugen
3 Chur	6 Chiavenna

4.9   IDEAS FOR REPORTS

Choose one of the following topics, or any other topic that interests you.
    First, *write down in ten minutes as many ideas on the subject as you can, (except in (f), where you will have to carry out a survey).*
    Then *look through all the ideas, and decide if there are some that are not particularly important or relevant, and can therefore be left out.*
    After that, *group the ideas that you have, and decide on the best order, both within each group and among the groups.*
    Finally, *bearing in mind the content of the whole report, write a suitable introduction and also a suitable conclusion.*

a) A report on flexible study hours in your school. (Compare 4.4.)
b) A report on eating habits intended to encourage people to eat more sensibly. (Compare 4.6.)
c) A report by an invalid on his or her first month using an invalid car provided by the Invalids' Transport Society. (Compare 4.7.)
d) A confidential report on someone who wants to become a social worker.
e) A report on the progress of a journey that you made, or of a historically famous journey, or of an imaginary journey. (Compare 4.8.)
f) Survey three books available in your country for teaching English to beginners. Write a report on them.
g) Report the various stages of a labour dispute, from early discontent through to a satisfactory solution.

5   Brochures and guides

5.1   PUNCTUATION

Compare the following pairs of examples. 1, 3, 5 and 7 have a full stop between the two sentences. A semicolon would also be possible, but not a comma. 2, 4, 6 and 8, on the other hand, have a comma. Working in groups of two or three, decide why 2, 4, 6 and 8 can have a comma.

1   Turn on the main switch. Then set the temperature gauge to 50°.
2   Turn on the main switch, and then set the temperature gauge to 50°.
3   The City is interesting on weekdays. On Sunday it is almost completely deserted.
4   The City is interesting on weekdays, but on Sunday it is almost completely deserted.
5   There is often a cool breeze in the evenings. Don't forget to pack a couple of jerseys.
6   There is often a cool breeze in the evenings, so don't forget to pack a couple of jerseys.
7   Seats can be booked through a ticket agency. They can also be purchased at the theatre.
8   Seats can be booked through a ticket agency, or they can be purchased at the theatre.

Now decide whether the following examples need any changes:

9   You can visit the famous buildings by bus, you can also take a horse-drawn cab.
10   The concerts usually start when the sun has gone down, they last for about two and a half to three hours.
11   We will spend part of the day by the sea, bring a swimsuit.
12   Our guides are all experienced, most of them speak several languages, in any case all of them speak English.
13   The bus leaves at 11 o'clock, we have lunch in a delightful little restaurant on top of the cliffs, then we visit the caves in the afternoon, finally we have a guided tour of the old town.
14   Munich is sometimes called the village with a million people, it is the capital of Bavaria, it has wonderful art museums and churches.

5.2 SCRAMBLED SENTENCES

The following sentences go together to form the text of a travel brochure, but they are in the wrong order. Working in groups of two or three, put them in the right order, and decide how the words and phrases in bold type help to link the text together. Then compare your answers with those of other groups.

a) For **these lucky ones** it's the beginning of an unforgettable air-sea holiday with the world's leading cruiser company: the Royal Seafaring Line.

b) **What's more,** our chefs will prepare food for you that is as varied as it is delicious; you will find it difficult to choose from the range of Caribbean and international specialities.

c) **So** don't delay – see your travel agent today!

d) Whether you choose **the relaxation on board or the stimulation on land,** you will have the holiday of a lifetime.

e) **So** you can relax on the vast sundeck, bide your time with a cocktail, or dance till dawn in the nightclub or in the discotheque.

f) For many of **the passengers it's** just a normal scheduled flight, but for some it's the start of something very special.

g) In Kingston, Jamaica's capital, **RSL's own cruiser** is waiting to introduce **them** to the unique world of the Caribbean.

h) While you can **thus** spend a perfect holiday without leaving the ship, there is **also** the **added** attraction of fascinating shore visits at each of our ports of call.

i) And **it's all** included in the price – just £1,995 for 21 days.

j) Every Tuesday a British Airways flight leaves Heathrow for Jamaica.

k) Like all our ships, **this cruiser** has been specially designed to give you maximum comfort, luxury and enjoyment.

5.3 LINKING WORDS AND PHRASES

In the following sentences the linking words and phrases are missing. Working in groups of two or three, choose the most appropriate word or phrase from the ones given. Then compare your answers with those of other groups.

1 Most of the interesting things take place on Saturday and Sunday.
   ...., a weekend is the best time for a visit.
   a) For example   b) Namely   c) I.e.   d) In other words

2 This film is for adults only, ... people over 16 years
   of age.
   a) such as   b) i.e.   c) e.g.

3 Fresh field mushrooms are readily available during only one season,
   .... the autumn.
   a) namely   b) for instance   c) in other words

4 For a baby, breast milk has many advantages over bottle milk.
   ...., it builds up the baby's defences against disease.
   a) I.e.   b) Namely   c) For example   d) In other words

5 Everybody takes part in the dancing, ..., everybody
   except the musicians.
   a) in other words   b) or rather   c) namely   d) for instance

6 Man-made fibres .... nylon and Terylene can be
   combined with cotton to give greater strength.
   a) such as   b) i.e.   c) namely   d) or rather

7 Universities and Colleges of Advanced Technology,
   ...., places of higher learning, are financed partly by
   the state and partly out of private funds.
   a) that is to say   b) for example   c) namely   d) e.g.

8 Some metals, ... platinum, are more expensive than
   gold.
   a) i.e.   b) such as   c) in other words   d) viz.

9 In August everyone goes away, ..., everyone not
   connected with the tourist industry.
   a) for example   b) i.e.   c) or rather   d) in other words

10 The town's traditional handicrafts depend on two materials,
    .... leather and silk.
    a) viz.   b) e.g.   c) such as   d) in other words

Now, working in groups of two or three, put an appropriate word or phrase in the following sentences to bring out the relationship between the parts.

11 There is only one town in England with more than five million inhabitants,
    .... London.

12 Late at night buses and trains can be dangerous. ....,
   if you want to avoid trouble, take a taxi.

13 The tour will include visits to several places of interest,
   ...., the British Museum and the Tower of London.

14 This brochure mainly concerns self-employed people,
   .... people who work but who are not employed by
   someone else.

15 A discount is given to students, ..., to people who
   have a students' card, which is not always the same.

Now, working individually, complete the following sentences with an appropriate word or phrase.

16 The offer in this brochure concerns only household appliances, i.e.
   ....

17 The offer in this brochure concerns only household appliances, e.g.
   ....

18 Foreigners often find the months of July and August much too hot. In other
   words, ...
   ....

19 Only two countries have sent people into space, viz. ....
   ....

20 I like all sorts of food, or rather, ...
   ....

21 Many large sea birds, such as ...., can stay in
   the air for very long periods of time.

22 There is only one metal that is liquid at room temperature, namely
   ....

23 Winter sports, e.g. ...., are very popular these
   days.

24 Good language schools, that is to say, ..., can
   afford to charge high prices.

5.4 PARAGRAPHS

Working in groups of two or three, divide the following brief introduction to London into paragraphs. Then write a similar brief introduction to a big city or a region that you know well, paying special attention to the division into paragraphs.

London has a great deal to offer visitors. Whether your tastes are modern or traditional, sophisticated or simple, there's plenty in London for you. Most visitors do some shopping, and there is an enormous range of possibilities, from the bargains of Petticoat Lane (Sunday morning) or Portobello Road (Saturday morning) to the jewellery and furs of Hatton Garden and Bond Street. A simple walk along Oxford Street will satisfy most ordinary needs or, if you want everything – from pins to pianos – under one roof, then Harrods is the shop for you. You will probably want to mix your shopping with a little sightseeing. You can visit the great buildings, such as St Paul's and Westminster Abbey, or you can watch the Changing of the Guard, or you can rest your feet in one of the large central parks, and all free. Not all the sightseeing is free, of course; you'll have to pay to go to the zoo in Regents Park, to see the Crown Jewels in the Tower, or for a boat trip along the Thames. Then there are the arts, both ancient and modern. The British Museum and the Victoria and Albert Museum have enormous collections of art and artefacts from many different countries, and the National Gallery in Trafalgar Square houses paintings by the old masters. The more modern world can be seen in the Science Museum, the Planetarium and in the paintings and sculptures of the Tate Gallery. In the evening, when you have walked far enough for one day, you can simply enjoy a drink in the atmosphere of a London pub. But if you want organised entertainment, you will always find a film, a concert or a play to interest you among the hundreds that are put on every day. Turning to the question of food, it must be admitted that the English have no great reputation as cooks, but visitors to London can savour food from all over the world: from Mexican to Russian, from Scandinavian to Japanese. In particular, there are hundreds of Indian, Pakistani, Chinese and Italian restaurants, most of which serve good, relatively cheap meals. This brief survey should give you some idea of the great variety of things to do in London. There is literally something for everyone at almost any time during the day. So, as a famous Londoner once said: 'When a man is tired of London, he is tired of life.'

5.5 SELECTION AND ORDERING

The following table gives some facts about three package holidays and their resorts. Write the text for a brochure recommending one of them either to families with young children or to young students. Working in groups of two or three, decide which facts to include, group them into paragraphs, decide on a suitable order of presentation, and then write the text.

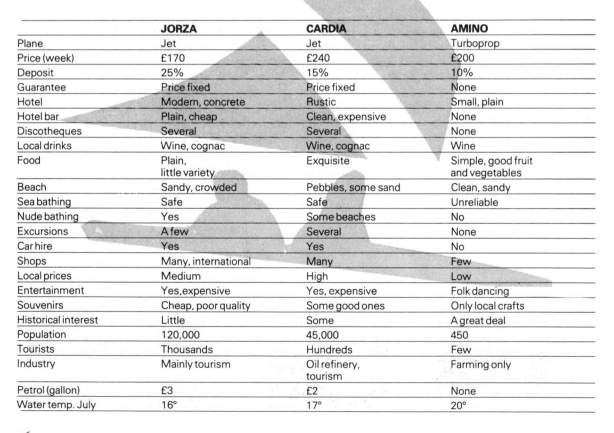

	JORZA	CARDIA	AMINO
Plane	Jet	Jet	Turboprop
Price (week)	£170	£240	£200
Deposit	25%	15%	10%
Guarantee	Price fixed	Price fixed	None
Hotel	Modern, concrete	Rustic	Small, plain
Hotel bar	Plain, cheap	Clean, expensive	None
Discotheques	Several	Several	None
Local drinks	Wine, cognac	Wine, cognac	Wine
Food	Plain, little variety	Exquisite	Simple, good fruit and vegetables
Beach	Sandy, crowded	Pebbles, some sand	Clean, sandy
Sea bathing	Safe	Safe	Unreliable
Nude bathing	Yes	Some beaches	No
Excursions	A few	Several	None
Car hire	Yes	Yes	No
Shops	Many, international	Many	Few
Local prices	Medium	High	Low
Entertainment	Yes, expensive	Yes, expensive	Folk dancing
Souvenirs	Cheap, poor quality	Some good ones	Only local crafts
Historical interest	Little	Some	A great deal
Population	120,000	45,000	450
Tourists	Thousands	Hundreds	Few
Industry	Mainly tourism	Oil refinery, tourism	Farming only
Petrol (gallon)	£3	£2	None
Water temp. July	16°	17°	20°

5.6   TEXT COMPARISON

Working in groups of two or three, decide which of the following guides to English towns you prefer, and why. Then discuss your decision with other groups. Then look again at the text you did not like; decide what you would change. (Invent any details you need.) Finally, working individually, write a better guide.

Chester

There are many features of historical interest in Chester. It was founded by the Romans, but Chester is also famous for its Tudor-style shopping centre called 'The Rows'. In an age when many municipal corporations are only beginning to introduce pedestrian precincts, it is interesting to note that 'The Rows' have been in existence for hundreds of years.

If we enter the city from the north, we are at once aware that this is truly a Roman city. I have walked along the Roman walls many times because I live quite close to them. The baths were actually heated, and the system employed was very similar to modern central heating techniques. The water is contained in a medium-sized pool, which is supported on pillars, leaving a hollow chamber, and the hot air so produced heated the water as it flowed through the chamber. As I say, I think it's just like central heating.

Other things that people like to visit in Chester are the museum and the cathedral, but I don't like either very much. I much prefer Chester Races. The winner last year was Freddy Searly riding Rum Cocktail, although I didn't back it.

There's an excellent zoo near Chester. Children love going to zoos, and so do many adults. I especially like gorillas, and I've taken some very good photos of them. I wish visitors wouldn't feed the animals. There are notices everywhere telling them not to.

The famous Roman city of St Albans is 30 miles north of London and can easily be reached by train or bus. The town, although small, is well worth a visit, and the following places are of particular interest to the tourist. First, there are the Roman remains of Verulamium and the Roman theatre, both situated in beautiful natural surroundings near a lake. Second, and close by, is the impressive, largely Norman cathedral, the second longest in Britain, and housing the remains of the first Christian martyr, St Alban. You can then stroll along old winding streets, like Fishpool and George Street, both lined with fine examples of Tudor and Georgian houses, and not far away is the clock tower, built in 1645. Last, but not least, no visitor should leave the city without dropping in to one of the numerous picturesque old pubs. So when your feet are tired, have a rest and a drink in The White Horse, or The Fighting Cock, or The Boot, all delightful reminders of an earlier, more leisurely age.

5.7   TEXT WITH A DIAGRAM

UNESCO is compiling a guide in English to the school system in different countries. Each section will include a diagram showing the main types of school and the main public examinations related to the age of the students; the accompanying text will include a general description of the subjects studied and the examinations taken. First look at the section about the British school system, and then, working in groups of two or three, draw a diagram and write the accompanying text for the section on your country's school system.

The British School System

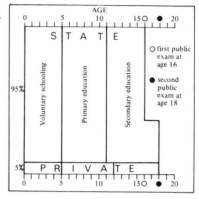

In Britain most schools are financed by the state and, for the children attending these schools, they are free. However, about 5 per cent of the school population attend private schools, and these are financed from pupils' fees. There are many local variations in the details of the school system – Scotland, in particular, has a system of its own which differs to quite an extent – but the general pattern of schooling in Britain is as follows.

All children must start school at the age of five. Many have previously attended play schools or nursery schools, but these are not compulsory. Primary education, whether state or private, seeks to develop all aspects of the child: physical and emotional, as well as intellectual and cultural. Different schools put different emphasis on academic success; most schools concentrate on the child's development of his or her potential, rather than on training for a particular exam. There is a tendency not to separate out traditional subjects, such as Geography, Religion, Music, etc, and instead to take an area of interest, for example a country or a century, and look at it from all possible points of view over a long period of time, perhaps as long as a week or two. A lot of the work is done in teams, thus fostering collaboration, and the pupils are encouraged to find things out for themselves.

Roughly at the age of 11 (but often somewhat later, especially in the case of private education), children move to different schools. These are called secondary schools, and nowadays most of them are comprehensive, that is to say, children of all abilities go to the same school. Within some comprehensive schools children are put into different classes according to their intellectual ability; in others, children of different abilities are all kept together in the same class.

In the first four or five years at a secondary school, the pupils have a set timetable of subjects, including arts subjects, such as History, English and a foreign language, as well as science subjects and sports. At the end of this period most pupils take one of two public examinations, though these do not normally include all the subjects that the students have studied. In fact, a pupil may take the exam in as many, or as few, subjects as is thought suitable.

After these exams, i.e. at the age of 16 or so, most pupils at state schools leave. Only about 30 per cent continue at school, compared with about 90 per cent in the small private sector. For those that stay on, in either type of school, the next two or three years are spent concentrating on a small number of subjects, e.g. Latin, French and English, or Maths, Physics and Chemistry, and so on. These specialist subjects take up more than half the pupils' timetable, and at the end of these years of concentrated preparation, the pupils usually take a public school-leaving examination in their three specialist subjects. Their results in these exams will largely determine whether they now start to work, or whether they can continue with higher education at a university or college.

5.8   IDEAS FOR BROCHURES AND GUIDES

Choose one of the following topics, or any other topic that interests you.
   First, *write down in ten minutes as many ideas on the subject as you can.*
   Then *look through all the ideas, and decide if there are some that are not particularly important or relevant, and can therefore be left out.*
   After that, *group the ideas that you have, and decide on the best order, both within each group and among the groups.*
   Now *compose each paragraph, linking the ideas together with suitable words and phrases.*
   Finally, *bearing in mind the content of the whole text, write a suitable introduction and a suitable conclusion.*

a) The text for a holiday brochure about a place where you have spent a holiday.
b) The text for a holiday brochure about an unusual type of holiday, e.g. pony-trekking, safari, grape-picking, etc. (Compare 5.2.)
c) A text intended to encourage people to visit your favourite restaurant, shop, bar, club, discotheque, museum or art gallery.
d) The text, with an accompanying diagram, for a guide to the university system in your country. (Compare 5.7.)
e) A brief guide to your country, region or town specifically intended for people interested in either (a) watching sport, or (b) playing sport, or (c) nature and wild life, or (d) art, or (e) architecture, or (f) history, or (g) food and drink, or (h) customs and traditions.

6 Articles

6.1 PUNCTUATION

Notice the use of the colon (:) in the following sentences. How are the first and second halves of each sentence related to one another? In what way are 1 and 2 different from 3 and 4?

1 We need the following: two boiling fowls, a kilo of potatoes and one large onion.
2 Only three elements are lighter than beryllium: hydrogen, helium and lithium.
3 The message was terse and to the point: the police have your description.
4 The whole thing became terribly clear: they had no means of escape.

Notice the use of the semicolon (;) in the following sentences. What are the ways in which the first half of each sentence is related to the second? Could the semicolon be replaced by a comma or a full stop? If so, what other change would be necessary, and would the effect be the same?

5 His first book was published in Britain; all his later ones were published in America.
6 One man went to mow; the others went to sow.
7 Last year at this time they were sailing round the world; now they are serving time in a top-security gaol.
8 At yesterday's auction the first three lots went to foreign buyers; all the others were bought by British collectors.

Compare the punctuation and meaning in the following sentences:

9 The equipment included a small motor, a transformer, two yards of wire and a switch.
10 The equipment included a small motor, which was fitted with a transformer, two yards of wire and a switch.
11 The equipment included a small motor, which was fitted with a transformer; two yards of wire; and a switch.

Sentences 1–4 above are typical examples of the use of the colon; sentences 5–8 and 11 are typical uses of the semicolon. Now, working in groups of two or three, suggest suitable punctuation for the following sentences:

12 The reason was obvious they could not afford the fare.
13 The summer is short and intense the winter is long but mild.
14 There were two obvious suspects Bryanston and Waites.

15 Each team was allowed the following 10 kilos of food including fruit water salt and ample petrol.

16 Each team was allowed the following 10 kilos of food including fruit water and salt and ample petrol.

17 The garden was decorated with coloured lamps the house itself was adorned with paper chains.

18 The estate consisted of a large forest complete with hunting lodge several meadows a lake and about 30 acres of arable land.

19 Yorkshire which was the largest county was split into three new administrative areas Rutland which was the smallest county was absorbed into the neighbouring area.

20 They made two important decisions the oldest houses would be pulled down the more recent ones would be repaired.

6.2   SCRAMBLED SENTENCES

The following sentences go together to form a complete newspaper article, but they are in the wrong order. Working in groups of two or three, put them in the right order, and decide how the words and phrases in bold type help to link the text together. Then compare your answers with those of other groups.

a) In a telephone call to the Daily Herald, the National Liberty Movement said they had placed **the bomb** in protest at the council's decision to ban all political demonstrations, but they regretted **the incidental damage**.

b) On being informed of **the explosion** and **the police investigations**, the mayor, Mr Jack Lambert, who is currently on holiday abroad, commented: 'This barbarous act is a sad reflection on the politics of today.'

c) **One** is aged about 35, with ginger hair, a beard and rimless glasses.

d) The council building, **however**, suffered considerable damage.

e) A right-wing extremist group has claimed responsibility for the bomb that exploded last night outside the council offices.

f) Witnesses have told the police that **both men** were wearing dark blue overalls and yellow anoraks.

g) **In addition**, windows were smashed in several nearby shops and offices.

h) **The other** is about 20, walks with a pronounced limp, and has long fair hair.

i) The police have issued a description of two men—thought to be **prominent NLM members**—whom they wish to interview in connection with the explosion.

j) **Furthermore**, one was carrying a suspiciously large plastic bag when they were seen in Main Square at about midnight.

k) **The explosion** took place at about 1 am when **the offices were empty, and there were therefore no casualties**.

6.3 LINKING WORDS AND PHRASES

In the following article on Nuclear Hazards the linking words and phrases are missing. Working in groups of two or three, choose the most appropriate word or phrase from the ones given. Then compare your answers with those of other groups.

There are three separate sources of hazard related to the use of nuclear reactions to supply us with energy. (1)......................... ...., the radioactive material must travel from its place of manufacture to the power station.(2).................................... the power stations themselves are solidly built, the containers used for the transport of the material are not. Unfortunately, there are normally only two methods of transport available, (3)..................................... road or rail, and both of these involve close contact with the general public, (4)............ ....the routes are bound to pass near, or (5).............................. ....through, heavily populated areas. (6)..., there is the problem of waste. All nuclear power stations produce wastes which in most cases will remain radioactive for thousands of years. It is impossible to de-activate these wastes, and (7)..................................... they must be stored in one of the ingenious but cumbersome ways that scientists have invented. (8).., they may be buried under the ground, dropped into disused mineshafts, or sunk in the sea.(9).., these methods do not solve the problem; they merely store it, (10)................................. .... an earthquake could crack open the containers like nuts.

(11)......................................., there is the problem of accidental exposure due to a leak or an explosion at the power station. As with the other two hazards, this is extremely unlikely and (12).................. .... does not provide a serious objection to the nuclear programme, (13) .... it can happen, as the inhabitants of Harrisburg will tell you.

Separately, and during short periods, these three types of risk are no great cause for concern. Taken together, (14).................. ...., and especially over much longer periods, the probability of a disaster is extremely high.

1   a) So   b) Firstly   c) Rather
2   a) Secondly   b) But   c) Although
3   a) for example   b) such as   c) namely
4   a) because of   b) although   c) since
5   a) even   b) for instance   c) on the other hand
6   a) Secondly   b) Thirdly   c) In that case
7   a) because   b) so   c) after
8   a) Besides   b) For example   c) However
9   a) By the way   b) Lastly   c) However
10 a) though   b) since   c) after
11 a) Thirdly   b) Also   c) For instance
12 a) so   b) instead   c) even
13 a) although   b) nevertheless   c) but
14 a) although   b) though   c) even though

Now write an article on pollution, using as many as possible of the words and phrases you have inserted in the article above.

6.4 FIRST AND LAST PARAGRAPHS

In the following article the first and last paragraphs are missing. After the article there are three alternatives for each. Working in groups of two or three, choose the most suitable first and last paragraph. Then compare your answers with those of other groups. What makes a good first paragraph? What makes a good last paragraph? How should they be related to the rest of the article?

(First paragraph missing)

The police say hundreds of offenders have been caught by Mrs Gordon, a citizen who writes down the licence numbers of people who break the law in this way, and sends them in to the local police station.

'Anyone can sign a ticket,' said a police officer, 'and she's signed a lot.'

A driver was heading down Clifton Avenue this morning, when she found herself stopped behind a school bus with its red lights flashing. Instead of stopping, the driver started to overtake the bus. But Mrs Gordon was on the spot, and warned her not to do it. However, the driver passed the bus anyway, and Mrs Gordon took her number.

Another driver received a summons in the mail after a similar incident a few weeks ago. When she entered the courtroom, she found Mrs Gordon there, notebook in hand. 'They tell me I should be a policewoman, but I don't want to be,' says Mrs Gordon. 'It's just that these people are breaking the law, and they shouldn't.'

Every weekday morning Mrs Gordon stands in front of the main supermarket, notebook and pencil at the ready, waiting to catch people passing school buses illegally. 'Nobody else wants to be bothered,' she says, 'but I won't just sit there twiddling my thumbs. I want to do something about it.' She began her personal campaign a year ago when her 13-year-old son Jack started taking the school bus.

But the job is getting harder. She used to give the police the licence numbers and sign a complaint, but now they want more evidence before they will act. She must now give a description of the car and the driver, as well as appear in court personally. A lot of people know she's there, and make a point of stopping, but she knows they wouldn't stop if she wasn't watching.

(Last paragraph missing)

Choices for first paragraph:

a) According to the law in New Merton, it is an offence for any driver to overtake a school bus when this has stopped with its red lights flashing. School buses make frequent stops to pick up and set down children on their way to and from school. This law is intended to reduce the number of accidents caused by children running across the road when they get off the bus.

b) Margaret Gordon is a one-woman police force, when it comes to motorists who illegally pass stopped buses. Thanks to her personal campaign, parts of New Merton have become safer for children. She takes down the number of any offender, and sends it to the police. But she's running into difficulties.

c) Margaret Gordon doesn't drive a car. She doesn't like publicity, and she doesn't like telling the police about people, but she often writes to the police, and the police sometimes take action. She hates traffic because the school buses stop, but the cars don't, so many motorists hate her.

Choices for last paragraph:

a) Mrs Gordon wears very nice clothes, and she is a pretty woman. I think it's a pity she has to do this all the time, don't you? I mean, it would be better if people obeyed the laws, and stopped behind the buses, but they don't. What do you think? Do you always stop when you see a school bus? I don't, I must admit, but I'm going to make a special effort to do so in the future. Why don't you?

b) In summary, Mrs Gordon has so far written 57 tickets in the space of six months. Of those, 39 have resulted in successful prosecutions and the payment of fines totalling over $400. Since there are about 80 school buses in operation, this means an average of about $5 per bus.

c) Mrs Gordon declined to be photographed. She said she didn't want angry motorists taking action in revenge. 'I don't particularly want people to pay fines,' she says. 'It's not that I like writing out tickets. I just want people to obey the law, that's all.'

6.5 SELECTION AND ORDERING

A new university is about to be built in a nearby town. The editor of a local newspaper has asked you to write a short article to tell his readers about the university. You have made the following notes of possible points to include. Working in groups of two or three, decide which points to include, and why the others should not be included. Discuss your decisions with other groups. Then group the points into paragraphs, and write each paragraph using suitable linking words and phrases. Finally, write a suitable first and last paragraph.

It will be a big university.
The university will teach all the principal arts and science subjects.
It will open four years from now.
The expected first year's intake of students is 7,500.
Modern universities are very important nowadays.
The university will give emphasis to the problems of developing countries, with a special Department of Third World Studies.
Five years after opening the student population is expected to have reached 25,000.
Students are expected to come from all parts of the country, just as with other British universities.
In the first years of its existence there will be the usual lack of funds and research facilities.
The University of Gotsby will be built three miles outside the village of Gotsby on a site near the golf course.
Gotsby has a large modern shopping centre and several cinemas and pubs.
It is hoped that there will be a maximum of 15 students in seminars and tutorials.
Not all the buildings will have been completed in time for inauguration, so to start with, some classes will be held in makeshift accommodation.

Flackerton University, 25 miles away, was built in 1860, and is not considered as a modern university any longer.

I went to London University and have a degree in English and History.

The inhabitants of Gotsby are worried that the village will be swamped by university students.

It will be a campus university, i.e. teaching and research rooms, shops, restaurants, entertainment and sports facilities, and halls of residence, etc., will all be part of the same total complex.

Some of the teaching staff will be old and experienced; some will be young.

The residents of Gotsby say that the university will create problems of accommodation, entertainment, transport, etc., in the village.

Campus-style universities are much more expensive than traditional British ones.

Many articles have recently been written about the problems of new universities.

The university will be financed partly by the state and partly by local business.

The Queen has declined to be the Rector of the new university.

There is expected to be a high demand for places, and many students will have to be rejected in the first few years.

6.6 TEXT BASED ON A CONVERSATION

The following report appeared in a local newspaper. It was written by a reporter who had interviewed a well-known explorer. After reading the report, look at the conversation between the same reporter and another local celebrity, this time a lone sailor. Working in groups of two or three, write a newspaper report based on the conversation with Derek Towers.

PERLBURY BOYS ROW UP AMAZON

Georgina Nugent reports on the incredible adventures of local boy Barry Minnerton, group leader at the Perlbury Outdoor Recreation Centre.

Barry has just returned from a six-week expedition in which he and four other young men, all from Perlbury, attempted to row up the Amazon. Unfortunately, the expedition was not completely successful, since their boats were wrecked in some very difficult rapids. Nevertheless, they had a fascinating trip, and Barry looks very fit. I asked him if he had felt afraid during the trip, and he laughed. He admitted that at the beginning he had been afraid of almost everything: of drowning, disease, insects, reptiles, and even the local Indians. But after two or three days they just got used to the danger and there was so much work to do that they didn't have time to worry.

In spite of all the hazards, Barry and his friends have set a new record by rowing up some four fifths of their projected route, and at the same time they learnt a great deal about local conditions and also about themselves. I asked Barry if he was planning to go back to the Amazon in the near future. He smiled and said, 'Not just yet.' First, he and his friends are going to have a well-earned rest, and then they intend to look for a larger, stronger boat.

I think that we should all be proud of having such an intrepid explorer in our town, and I trust that your readers will join me in congratulating Barry and his friends, and in wishing them all the best for the future.

G: Well, it's Derek Towers! Fancy seeing you here! I haven't seen you for months. Where've you been?

D: I've been sailing.

G: What? In the middle of winter? You must be mad!

D: It isn't cold all over the world, you know.

G: Listen, Derek. Exactly where have you been?

D: Well, as a matter of fact, I've just come back from the West Indies.

G: You sailed back?

D: No, I came back by plane, but I sailed *there* in a 30-foot yacht. I didn't have time to sail back because I wanted to be home for Christmas.

G: Were you on holiday then, or what?

D: No, well, I suppose I was. But I was trying to break the single-handed record. I'm afraid I didn't quite make it though. Bad weather, I'm afraid.

G: You mean, you went across the Atlantic by yourself in a 30-foot boat?

D: Yes, but it's not so difficult. Lots of people are doing it nowadays.

G: Well, how long did it take you?

D: Thirty days, I'm afraid. Very slow compared with what I was hoping for.

G: Didn't you find it very difficult to stay awake for all that time?

D: Good lord! You can't stay awake for thirty days! Even lone sailors need a few hours' sleep every night.

G: Well, who steers the boat at night, then?

D: Automatic steering. You just set your course and the sails, and it works with the wind. Like a sort of wind vane.

G: And what happens if the wind changes?

D: You instinctively notice the change in the movement of the boat, and you wake up.

G: But there's no one keeping a lookout for other boats. Isn't that dangerous?

D: Well, yes, I suppose it is. But the chances of a collision are very small, and even then I hope I'd wake up before anything serious happened.

G: Weren't you frightened at all?

D: I think when you go sailing, especially when you are alone, you experience a whole range of emotions: fear, depression, apathy, joy, even great peace. And, of course, physical exhaustion.

G: Why do you do it then?

D: I've no idea. At the time it's very hard, and you say to yourself 'never again', but when you get back on land again, you always want to return to the sea. It's like a sort of addiction.

G: Are you going to try again soon?

D: Let me have a bit of a rest first. Ask me again after Christmas.

6.7 ARTICLE BASED ON VISUAL INFORMATION

The following article, with an accompanying graph, explains the incidence of reports of sightings of unidentified flying objects (UFOs) in the State of Iowa. Read it; then, working in groups of two or three, underline the words and phrases which correspond to the different parts of the graph. Finally, write an article to accompany the second graph, which describes the progress of a virus epidemic.

UNIDENTIFIED FLYING OBJECTS IN THE STATE OF IOWA

During the early part of January of this year the rate of UFO reports was steady at around three or four a week. On Monday 16 January, however, CBB put out a science fiction film about visitors from outer space, and there was an immediate sharp increase in reports of sightings from all parts of the state. In the course of the following two weeks the number of reports gradually declined. Nevertheless, the commanding officer of Tawukee Airforce Base, General Wayne Tailor, who is directly responsible for the investigation of all such reports, decided to make his findings known. Accordingly, on Monday 30 January the Iowa Chronicle carried an article written by Tailor, which maintained that all UFO reports could be explained quite naturally as due to civil and military aircraft movements.

Following this explanation there was a rapid drop in the number of reported sightings, although the rate did not return to the pre-broadcast level.

Some people, though, were not convinced. One sceptic was Martin Hogarty, science correspondent of the Iowa Herald. On Friday 16 February Hogarty published a highly critical piece about the airforce, claiming that they were trying to cover up, and demanding an independent enquiry. This article caused a renewal of interest in the subject of UFOs and a corresponding steep rise in the number of reported sightings,

although this was not as marked as the increase in January.

General Tailor at once invited Hogarty to meet him in a public debate ten days later. CBB apparently felt they owed the commander an apology for the trouble they had caused him, and consequently they agreed to screen the debate. Inexplicably, Hogarty did not show up on the day, and it was left to the commander to produce some very convincing evidence for his case.

As a result, interest in UFOs fell right down to rock bottom: sightings were even lower than at the beginning of the year. As the weeks went by there was a slight increase in the number of reports, but this only brought the rate back to the normal level of 3 or 4 per week, where it has remained up to the present.

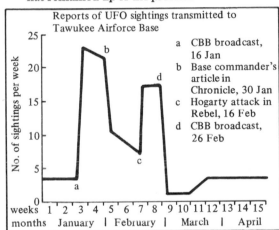

Reports of UFO sightings transmitted to Tawukee Airforce Base

a   CBB broadcast, 16 Jan
b   Base commander's article in Chronicle, 30 Jan
c   Hogarty attack in Rebel, 16 Feb
d   CBB broadcast, 26 Feb

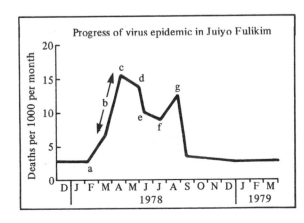

Progress of virus epidemic in Juiyo Fulikim

a) Return of a small group of migrant workers from an infected area.
b) Very dry spring; lack of drinking water.
c) Quarantine measures introduced by government.
d) WHO sends limited supplies of medicine.
e) Medicine loses effectiveness; reasons unknown.
f) Doctors recognise a virulent strain that resists treatment.
g) Vaccine produced; population vaccinated.

6.8   ARTICLE ON CLASSIFICATION

The following is an article about the different types of British newspapers. What different phrases does the writer use to indicate that he is changing to a different aspect of the topic? All these phrases serve the same purpose, so why does he use a different phrase each time?

BRITISH NEWSPAPERS

BRITISH NEWSPAPERS can be classified into g r o u p s according to various criteria, such as area of distribution, size of sales, socioeconomic class of their readers, days (and times) of publication, and political bias. Each of these different criteria will lead to more or less different group-ings.

With regard to the area of distribution, a fairly clear dis-tinction can be made between national p a p e r s and local papers. The nationals, e.g. The Times, the Daily Mirror, the Sunday Express, are readily obtainable in virtually all parts of the United Kingdom at the same time. On the other hand, local papers, e.g. the Yorkshire Post or the Liverpool Echo, serve a particular area, and outside that area must be specially ordered.

As regards the sales figures, we must recognize that there is no clear line that will distin-guish between large and small sales. However, we make a somewhat arbitrary distinction here, partly based on copies sold, but also influenced by the type of content of the papers. This separates the so-called 'popular' papers from the 'quality' papers; the 'quali-ties', like The Sunday Times or the Financial Times, tend to have l o n g e r, more serious articles than the 'populars', such as The People or the News of the World. In general, the 'popular' papers appeal to a larger audience t h a n the 'quality' papers and, as a con-sequence, they have larger sales. The major exception to this division is the Daily Tele-graph, which is 'quality' in the sense of having long, serious articles, but 'popular' in the sense that it sells well in ex-cess of a million copies a day.

Regarding the socioeconomic class of the readers, a classifi-cation on these lines will to a large extent reflect the above distinction into quality and popular. This is because the quality papers are mostly in-tended for the upper income groups, w h i l e t h e popular papers find their r e a d e r s among the lower socioecon-omic groups. Thus, a reader of The Observer or the Finan-cial Times, which are quality papers, is likely to be an educated person with quite a good income, while a reader of the Daily Mail or The Sun is more likely to be a less well-educated person with a lower income. This is obviously a broad generalisation, for although in the main it follows the facts, it is nevertheless true that a more detailed study would show that the complete picture is somewhat more complicated.

As to the days of publication, most British papers are either so-called 'daily papers', (which in fact do not appear on Sun-days), e.g. The Guardian or The Scotsman, or Sunday papers, like The Sunday Times or the News of the World. Local papers with small circulations, however, might appear only once or twice a week, or even less frequently, depending on the demand for them. Concern-ing the time of publication, the vast majority are morning papers, i.e. they go on sale early in the morning, while the minority are the so-called 'evening' papers, whose sales might start as early as midday, and then continue until the evening.

From the political point of view, British newspapers are not party organs, that is to say, they are not owned by one of the political parties and ex-pected to support its views unquestioningly. However, all the papers have a more or less clear political bias, and the great majority of the British press falls at some point be-tween the centre and the right of the political spectrum. Of the sixteen daily and Sunday national papers, only four, namely the Daily Mirror, the Sunday Mirror, The Sun and The People, are fairly con-sistent in their support of the Labour Party. Of the others, all but one purport to be neutral or tend to support, with varying degrees of enthus-iasm, the Conservative Party; the exception, The Guardian, usually gives loyal support to the Liberal Party.

Thus, while all papers have certain individual characteris-tics, it is still possible to classify them into different groupings according to certain general features which they share with others.

Now write an article about the different types of newspapers or magazines in your country, or about different types of games, or sports, or hobbies, or countries, or films, or holidays or jobs. Working in groups of two or three, first decide on a topic, and make a list of all the different ways in which it can be categorised. Write one paragraph for each, beginning each one with a phrase that shows you are changing the subject. Then write a suitable first and last paragraph.

6.9 IDEAS FOR ARTICLES

Choose one of the following topics, or any other topic that interests you.

First, *write down in ten minutes as many ideas on the subject as you can.*

Then *look through all the ideas, and decide if there are some that are not particularly important or relevant, and can therefore be left out.*

After that, *group the ideas that you have, and decide on the best order, both within each group and among the groups.*

Now *compose each paragraph, linking the ideas together with suitable words and phrases.*

Finally, *bearing in mind the content of the whole article, write a suitable introduction and a suitable conclusion.*

a) A newspaper report about an incident involving terrorists or freedom fighters. (Compare 6.2.)
b) An article on alternative sources of energy, i.e. other than oil or coal, and their problems. (Compare 6.3.)
c) A story about someone who does something unusual, and who is disliked for it. (Compare 6.4.)
d) An article about recent changes in the roles of men and women in your country.
e) A short article on the advantages and disadvantages of:
   a package holiday compared with independent travel, or
   records compared with cassettes, or
   private enterprise compared with public enterprise, or
   supermarkets compared with small shops.
f) An article on how to learn to cook, or to play a musical instrument, or to ski, or to learn a foreign language.

7 Instructions

7.1 PUNCTUATION

In the following recipe, note the use of commas (,) and full stops (.). Working in groups of two or three, try to explain why commas would be unsatisfactory instead of the full stops.

Pancake mixture ✌✌

Ingredients:
200 grams flour	100 grams butter
2 eggs	salt
4 decilitres milk	allspice

Sift the flour into a deep bowl, and add a little allspice and a pinch of salt. Beat the egg lightly, and put it in the mixture. Now add a little milk, and work the mixture into a thick paste without any lumps. Continue adding the milk little by little, but each time be sure to stir the mixture well so as to keep an even texture. When all the milk has been added, melt the butter, and stir it well into the mixture. It is now ready for use, but it will improve if it is left to stand for about half an hour.

Now, working individually, put commas and full stops in the appropriate places in the following recipe. Then compare your version with those of others.

Liver stew ✌✌

Ingredients:
400 grams lamb's liver	stock cube
2 large onions	flour
4 large carrots	oil
2 cloves of garlic	marjoram
300 grams of	sweet paprika
ripe tomatoes	black pepper

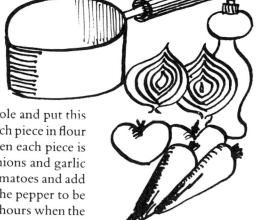

Put a cupful of hot water and a stock cube in a deep casserole and put this on a low heat sprinkle salt over the pieces of liver and dip each piece in flour fry the liver briefly in hot oil so as to seal in the juices when each piece is brown transfer it to the casserole now chop the carrots onions and garlic and put them in the casserole remove the skins from the tomatoes and add the juice to the other ingredients season to taste but leave the pepper to be added towards the end simmer on a low heat for about 1 ½ hours when the stew is ready to serve grind the black pepper over it

7.2 SCRAMBLED SENTENCES

The following sentences go together to form a set of instructions, but they are in the wrong order. Working in groups of two or three, put them in the right order, and decide how the words and phrases in bold type help to link the text together. Then compare your answers with those of other groups.

a) It is **also** a good idea **at this point** to check that the gas cylinder isn't empty.

b) **This,** of course, allows the gas to come through the pipe to the heater.

c) And then it's ready to go!

d) **When you then release it,** the pilot light should stay on.

e) Turn **this** to PILOT, and hold it down.

f) Lighting a calor gas heater is easy and safe if you follow these simple instructions.

g) It will light, but **keep the starter button pressed down** for about ten seconds.

h) **If it does,** then all you have to do is to turn the starter button **from PILOT** to ON.

i) **To start with,** make sure that everything is switched off.

j) **Now,** turn the tap on the top of the gas cylinder to ON.

k) **At the same time** hold a match through **the hole above** to the small pilot flame inside.

l) On the front of **the heater itself** you will find the starter button.

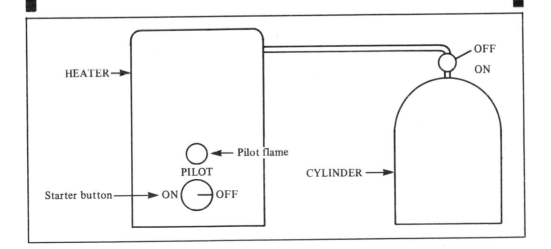

7.3   REPORTING WORDS

There are two reported speech versions of the following direct speech. Working in groups of two or three, decide which you prefer, and why. In particular consider the role of the reporting word ask. *Then discuss your conclusion with other groups.*

'I'd be really pleased,' said Betty, 'if you could find the time to help me.'

a) Betty said that she would be really pleased if I could find the time to help her.
b) Betty asked me to help her.

Now report the following items of direct speech, choosing in each case one of the reporting words given. Then compare your answers with those of others.

beg; allow; refuse; forbid; order; warn; encourage; suggest; dare; urge.

1   'Why don't you make a cake?' said Yvonne. 'I'm sure it would turn out, Tony, because you know how good you are at anything practical. I'm sure you'd find it quite easy, and in any case I'd give you a hand.'
2   'Jones!' said the headmaster. 'Pick up those papers at once!'
3   'Please, please say you'll help me,' Fred said. 'I'll do anything you want, but please help me this once, Jane.'
4   'All right. The boys can go home,' said Miss Pritchard.
5   'Don't go too near the edge, children,' said Mr Bream. 'You can easily slip there if you're not careful and that can be quite dangerous.'

Now choose two or three of the reporting words that you have not so far used; write examples of direct speech and reported speech to illustrate the use of these words.

7.4   PARAGRAPHS

The following is a detailed explanation of how to light a cigarette. After reading it, write a detailed explanation of how to do some simple everyday operation, such as:

boiling an egg   *cleaning your teeth*
making coffee or tea   *cleaning your shoes*
making an omelette   *bathing a dog.*

Before starting, make sure that you are not in a place where smoking is forbidden. Then take a cigarette out of the packet, and put the end to the mouth, holding it between the lips. After that, take a match out of the box, and close the box. Now strike the match along the side of the box until it bursts into flame. Next hold the flame to the end of the cigarette, and breathe in. When you are sure that the cigarette is lit, put the match out.

7.5 TEXT COMPARISON

The following letters contain instructions. Working in groups of two or three,
decide which you prefer, and why. Then discuss your decision with other
groups. Finally, rewrite the letter that you did not like.

Porky Farm
Hogshead
Berkshire

3 June 1982

Dear John,

As we agreed in our telephone conversation last week, here
are the instructions for what to do when you arrive at the farm.

First of all, collect the keys from the post office in the village. (We
always leave them there when we go away for a short time, and
they'll be expecting you.) The larger key is for the main door, and the
smaller one for the outhouses.

When you enter the house, the mains electricity switch is clearly
marked on the wall on your left. Turn it to ON, and make sure that
all the switches next to it are down in the ON position.

In order to connect the water supply, turn on the large red tap
which you will find below the sink in the bathroom. Note that the
water will take at least an hour to come through at full force.

Wood for the fires is in the outhouse beside the garage. Take
all the wood you need, but be careful to shut the door carefully
when you go out again, or the wood quickly gets damp and is
difficult to light.

Feed the chickens twice a day, morning and evening. Grain, bran
and old bread are in clearly marked containers by the front door.
Each morning collect the bowls from the hen run, and fill one with
a fresh mash of one part bread, one part left over vegetable peel,
food, etc, from the previous day, and one part bran. Also give them
clean water, and in the afternoon a bowlful of grain. As your
reward, don't forget to collect the eggs from the nesting boxes
every day, and enjoy them, too!

Before leaving the farm on the 22nd, make sure all the
switches and taps are turned off, and the windows and doors
securely locked. Check also that the chickens have full bowls
of water, grain and mash.

And please remember to return the keys to the post office, too!

Well, have a lovely time, and thank you once again for standing
in for us.

Love Mary

Flat 5,
St. Martins Court,
London.
N8

3 July 1982

Dear Mr & Mrs Levy,

Both my wife and I are happy to know that the documents are now all signed, and that you will definitely be coming to stay in our house next month as part of the International House Exchange Scheme. We are greatly looking forward to our stay in your home in New Jersey, and to seeing something of the USA. As requested, here are the instructions for what to do when you arrive.

You can pick up the keys from the Scheme office when you get to London. There will be three of them. Don't forget, please, to lock all the doors when you leave. Burglars, you know. The Thornes on the 3rd Floor – or is it the 4th? I can never remember – had their flat broken into recently. Oh, yes, and some of the plants are on the balcony. Anyway the main switch for turning on the water is in the kitchen. By the way, use any utensils you want. The central heating switch is also easy to find, too. Of course, if it's really hot, as it can be in London in August – like last year, for instance – then you won't want to bother. But it's there under the stairs if we have one of those Augusts like we had in 1976. When you leave, you can return the keys to the porter instead of to the Scheme office. That'll be easier for you, because he is in the block most of the time, except when he goes to see his sister who lives in Maidenhead. He's a very nice man, though a bit deaf, so you might have to shout. (His wife died recently too, poor thing.) Please don't forget to water all the plants, especially the ones outside on the balcony, as I mentioned. As I say, the water system and the central heating should cause you no problem, and you'll have no trouble in finding clean bed linen. Incidentally, we usually water the plants in the morning, before the sun comes round. On the other hand, the washing machine can be a bit tricky if you're not used to it, and it's beside the fridge. You'll need to switch on the electricity, of course, as soon as you arrive, so you won't have to worry about that. The key for the garage will be with Arnold Gold on the first floor, and be careful with the garage door, because it sometimes sticks. He might also be the best person to ask if you have any difficulty with the washing machine. Well, I hope I've remembered everything, but if I haven't, please write again and ask any questions that you've got.

Yours
Peter Rogers

P.S. Everything will be switched off when you get here because we're leaving England two weeks before you arrive.

7.6   TEXT BASED ON A VISUAL

Look at the diagram of the cassette recorder. Then read the instructions on how to record your voice.

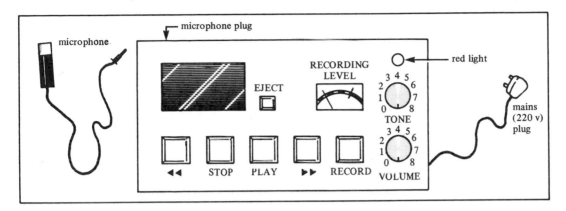

Instructions for recording your voice

1   First make sure that the set is plugged in to the mains (220 volts).
2   Then plug the microphone cable into the hole marked MICROPHONE at the back of the set.
3   Open the cassette lid by pressing the button marked EJECT.
4   Holding the cassette with the tape towards you, and with the tape on the left-hand spool, place the cassette in the machine.
5   Close the cassette lid.

6   Turn the recorder on by turning the VOLUME switch clockwise, and set it at about 6; the TONE button should be set at about 5.
7   Now press down the RECORDING button and the PLAY button at the same time. The red light should now come on, and the tape should start moving.
8   Test the volume level by saying a few words into the microphone, paying attention to the reaction of the RECORDING LEVEL indicator. If the needle goes past the red line, lower the volume; if the needle moves very little, increase the volume.

Now write complete instructions for the washing machine in the diagram to wash clothes – not very dirty ones – that are labelled:

> This garment of pure wool should be washed with soap flakes, not detergent, and no bleach, in tepid water. It should not be spun, but dried flat.

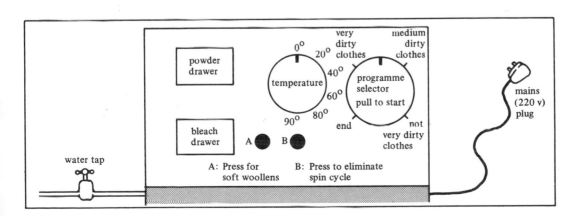

7.7   IDEAS FOR INSTRUCTIONS

Choose one of the following topics, or any other topic that interests you.

First, *write down in ten minutes as many ideas on the subject as you can.*

Then *look through all the ideas, and decide if there are some that are not particularly relevant or important, and can therefore be left out.*

After that, *group the ideas that you have, and decide on the best order, both within each group and among the groups.*

Now *compose each paragraph, linking the ideas together with suitable words and phrases.*

Finally, *bearing in mind the content of the whole, write a suitable introduction and a suitable conclusion.*

a) One of your favourite recipes. (Compare 7.1.)
b) Instructions, with a diagram, for a machine or apparatus that you know well, such as a record player or a camera. (Compare 7.2, 7.6.)
c) Someone is going to borrow your house or flat while you are away, but you will not be able to talk to them. Write careful instructions for them concerning all the things they will need to know. (Compare 7.5.)
d) Instructions for someone who is going to look after your garden, or your pet, or your young son or daughter. The instructions and explanations should be clear and simple, and they should take into account different circumstances that might arise.
e) Instructions for someone who is used to an automatic drive car about how to get from standstill up to top speed, and how to slow down and stop, in a car with normal gears.

8 Writing a story

8.1 PUNCTUATION

Notice the punctuation in the following sentences:

1 'We're going, and you're staying,' she said.
2 She said, 'We're going, and you're staying.'
3 'We're going,' she said, 'and you're staying.'
4 'We didn't play badly. In fact, we won,' Dolly replied.
5 'We didn't play badly,' replied Dolly. 'In fact, we won.'
6 Dolly replied, 'We didn't play badly. In fact, we won.'
7 'Who are you?' shouted the old woman.
8 The old woman shouted, 'Who are you?'
9 'Get out!' he screamed.
10 He screamed, 'Get out!'

Now, working in groups of two or three, punctuate the following sentences:

11 Did John come asked Michael
12 We are she insisted the oldest family around here
13 Leave me alone he roared
14 Then Mrs Smith asked where on earth were they
15 They've gone replied the countess and they won't be coming back
16 It's very nice she said quietly where did you buy it
17 I'd simply like to know my neighbour whispered where the woman lives
18 Yes, I do I said in a loud voice
19 Well he mumbled I don't really know what to say
20 The farmer shouted what the hell are you doing in there

Now, working individually, punctuate the following sentences:

21 I might come with you she said where exactly are you going
22 They're all out replied the maid and I've no idea when they'll be back
23 What my mother shouted don't you dare say that again
24 The old man whispered I can't really go very fast where can I sit down
25 No she said I'm afraid I can't do anything for you
26 What's your telephone number Susan asked with a smile

8.2   SCRAMBLED SENTENCES

The following sentences go together to form a story, but they are in the wrong order. Working in groups of two or three, put them in the right order, and decide how the words and phrases in bold type help to link the text together. Then compare your answers with those of other groups.

a)   **But** the strange thing is that nobody seems to live there.

b)   **It** is a large two-storey house with an ample garden.

c)   I don't like to stand **there and stare in,** but even a quick glance tells you that everything is **perfectly kept.**

d)   Or **is it?**

e)   Along the street from where I live is a house that is something of a mystery.

f)   **But** no one that I know **can.**

g)   **The** garden is neat and tidy, and **the** house itself is freshly painted and clean.

h)   Perhaps the people who live opposite could clarify **the point.**

i)   From when **they** leave until **their** next visit, the house is completely empty.

j)   **This** is surrounded by a high wall, and the only spot where you can see inside is the gate.

k)   **The only people you ever see** are the gardener and the house-keeper, who come early in the morning two or three times a week, and go away in the late afternoon.

8.3   LINKING WORDS AND PHRASES

In the following story the linking words and phrases are missing. Working in groups of two or three, decide which of the given words and phrases link the text sensibly together. Notice that in some cases more than one of the suggestions is possible. *Then compare your answers with those of other groups.*

Last summer my husband and I rented a cottage for two weeks.
(1) ...., we had always spent our summer holidays camping, either in England or abroad. (2) .... some of our friends had rented the same cottage the year before, we knew that the place would be clean and comfortable, and (3) .... near the beach.

(4) ...., the day before we left home the long-range weather forecast sounded good, which made us feel even more certain of a pleasant holiday.

(5) ...., our high hopes were soon dashed.

(6) ...., our problems started (7) .... we arrived, which was just after midnight. When we unlocked the door to the cottage, we found water everywhere; and we soon discovered the lights weren't working, (8) .... we spent the first night in the car. Fortunately, we managed to find an electrician and a plumber early the next day, and by midday all our problems were over, (9) ...., they *seemed* to be over. True, the things in the house were now in working order, but these turned out to be the least of our problems; much more important was what we came to call our 'invasions'.

(10) ...., there were the flies, which stayed with us for the whole fortnight. (11) .... there were the ants, with their annoying habit of getting into everything, (12) .... the fridge. (13) ...., like the flies, kept us constant company. (14) .... these permanent invasions, there were (15) .... shortlived ones. One night, (16) ...., the house was invaded (if that's the right word) by a mouse, (17) .... not for long. A bat was another unwelcome visitor; and (18) .... – but by no means least – we had a brief visit from a snake. That, (19) ...., was our cottage holiday. In all our experience as campers, we have never had any trouble with insects or animals, (20) .... once with some cows, and now we are wondering why we ever chose any other kind of holiday. Next year we'll go back to camping!

1   a) Previously   b) Beforehand   c) Before that
2   a) As   b) Since   c) For   d) Because of
3   a) also   b) too   c) as well
4   a) What's more   b) Moreover   c) On the other hand
5   a) Although   b) On the contrary   c) On the other hand
    d) However
6   a) To begin with   b) In fact   c) Instead
7   a) as early as   b) the moment   c) as soon as
8   a) so   b) therefore   c) then
9   a) as if   b) at last   c) or rather
10 a) At first   b) First   c) To begin with   d) At the beginning
11 a) Then   b) So   c) Even
12 a) even   b) also   c) including   d) i.e.
13 a) These   b) Those
14 a) Meanwhile   b) Apart from   c) Besides
15 a) also   b) even   c) in addition
16 a) for instance   b) e.g.   c) for example
17 a) though   b) but   c) except   d) in spite of that
18 a) at last   b) last   c) in the end   d) at the end
19 a) in brief   b) in short   c) in other words
20 a) although   b) including   c) except   d) but

8.4   REPORTING WORDS

There are two reported speech versions of the following direct speech. Working in groups of two or three, decide which you prefer, and why. In particular consider the role of the reporting word threaten. *Then discuss your conclusion with other groups.*

'Look here, Sue!' said Peter. 'If you don't stop annoying me, I'll hit you.'

a) Peter threatened to hit Sue because she was annoying him.
b) Peter told Sue to look there, and he said that if she didn't stop annoying him, he would hit her.

Now report the following items of direct speech, choosing in each case one of the reporting words given. Then compare your answers with those of others.

promise; intend; complain; remind; explain; suspect; offer; admit; doubt; remember.

1 'It's not fair,' said Fanny. 'Why does the company have to treat me so badly? These sort of things never happen to anybody else.'
2 'Oh, it's just occurred to me,' said Anne. 'It's my mother's birthday.'
3 'You remember how to get to the park, don't you?' Kate said. 'Just get the 45 bus, and get off at the top of the hill.'
4 'Of course, I'll never be able to prove it,' Mr Jackson said, 'but I bet it was the neighbours that told the police.'
5 Nellie said, 'If you like, I'll feed the children and put them to bed, and then you can go out for the evening.'

Now choose two or three of the reporting words that you have not so far used; write examples of direct speech and reported speech to illustrate the use of these words.

8.5   FIRST AND LAST SENTENCES

In the following paragraph the first and last sentences are missing. Working in groups of two or three, choose the most suitable suggestion from the ones given below. Then compare your answers with those of other groups.

....

....

We got to London at about 10 o'clock, and they were at the station to meet us. We got the tube, and chatted all the way to South Kensington. That's where the museums are, and we had already decided that we wanted to go there. So Rosemary went to the Science Museum with Uncle Peter, and I went to the Victoria and Albert Museum with Aunt Jill. Aunt Jill explained lots of interesting things to me, and apparently Rosemary had a good time, too. When we came out, though, we were all tired and hungry, and they took us to a super

French restaurant nearby. In the afternoon we were still too tired to walk anywhere, so we went to the latest disaster film. It was ever so expensive – Aunt Jill paid, thank goodness! – but the cinema was enormous, and the seats were really comfortable. If the film hadn't been exciting, I think I would have fallen asleep! After that we just had time to do a bit of shopping before it was time to rush off back to the station. ....
....
....

Choices for first sentence:

a) Rosemary and I sometimes go to London to visit our relatives, see the museums, and so on.
b) There are so many things to do in London, especially if you have relatives there.
c) Last Saturday Rosemary and I had a marvellous day in London with Aunt Jill and Uncle Peter.
d) Uncle Peter and Aunt Jill live in London, and they're quite well off, I think.

Choices for last sentence:

e) Aunt Jill and Uncle Peter haven't got any children of their own, but they are quite well off.
f) So, as you can see, it was a very interesting day in the capital for both of us.
g) That was the second time I'd been to London; the first time was two years ago.
h) The trains go about every hour, except on Sundays, and the journey takes an hour and a half.

Now, working individually, complete the following paragraph, for which you have only the first and last sentences:

But the best thing about the holiday was the couple we met by accident on the beach ....
....
....
....
....
....
....
....
....
....
.... I hope that gives you some idea why we enjoyed being with them so much.

8.6   TEXT COMPARISON

Working in groups of two or three, decide which of the following stories you prefer, and why. Then discuss your answer with those of other groups. Finally, write a similar story, based on the one you prefer, in which you describe your escape from the top floor of a burning building.

A   I climbed out of the submarine, the sea roared, at that moment the waves were enormous, they towered above me. I looked down, it was all black, I looked ahead, there was no light. The waves roared again, I was frightened, I decided to jump into the water. I knew it was cold, it was a difficult decision. I jumped in, I sank down. The waves poured over me, I didn't know which way I was going, I was thrown about, I lost my sense of direction. I could feel a terrible chill, I could feel it in all parts of my body, it was like a knife. I made a decision, I swam towards the others, then they were all around me, I could see them now. I felt comforted, my fear disappeared, there were other people around.

B   Just as I climbed out of the submarine, the sea gave a tremendous roar, and I could see the enormous waves towering above me. I looked down, and everything was black; there was no light to be seen ahead, either. The waves roared again, and I was suddenly very afraid. I had to make a move, though, so I leapt into the water, ignoring the fact that it was cold, and I immediately sank down as the waves poured over me.

   At first I was so thrown about I didn't know which way I was moving, and I lost all sense of direction. I began to feel a terrible chill which stabbed at every part of my body like a knife. I decided to try to swim towards where the others might be, and soon I could see them around me. The sight of them comforted me, and my fear disappeared as I realised I was no longer alone.

8.7   TEXT BASED ON A CONVERSATION

You have been staying in your parents' house while they are working abroad. You arrived home last night to find the house burgled, and you had the following conversation with the policeman who came to investigate. Write a letter to your parents telling them what has happened.

P: Good evening, sir. I've come to investigate the burglary that you phoned about. Now can you tell me what you know about it?
A: Well, for a start, this isn't my house. I'm just staying here for 6 months while my parents are working in Japan. So, apart from a few obvious things, like the radio, the TV, the stereo, the records and some paintings, I don't really know what else has gone. All the drawers have been emptied. God knows what my parents kept in them, or what they'll say when they know!
P: Yes, that will be a bit of a problem for you. Now . . .
A: I mean, it's not as if it was my fault. All the doors were locked, and the windows properly closed. I even left the hall light on to give the impression that someone was in, but I'm sure my father will think I'm responsible.

P: You'll just have to break the news to him gently, sir. Now, how exactly did you discover the burglary?

A: I went out at eight, as I do every Thursday, to go to my Italian class at the Institute in Roland Street. Afterwards I went to The Black Lion for a drink, and I got back here just after half past ten.

P: How can you be so sure of the time?

A: 'Cos I stayed in the pub until closing time, and it's only a two-minute walk from here.

P: I see. And what did you find when you got back here?

A: All this mess you can see around you. I just walked in through the front door, and found this. And it's the same upstairs – everything smashed, drawers emptied and thrown about. It's like an earthquake!

P: And do you know how the burglars got in?

A: Yes, the lock on the kitchen door has been forced.

P: And have you spoken to the neighbours? Perhaps they saw or heard something.

A: No, I haven't. But Mr Jones, on that side, is stone deaf and sits glued to the telly all evening, and the Richards, on the other side, are away.

P: Well, how soon could you let us know exactly what has been stolen?

A: I suppose I'll have to write and tell my parents straightaway. They're not due back until next month, but they'll almost certainly come back early when they hear about this.

P: I'd be pleased if you could contact them as soon as possible. You see, we can't really begin a full investigation till we know exactly what is missing.

A: I suppose there's not much chance of anything being recovered before my parents get to know, is there? My father is a stereo maniac. He'll go crazy when he hears that his stereo and the whole of his record collection has gone.

P: No, I shouldn't think there's much chance that we'll find anything soon, and perhaps not at all. These days there are so many burglaries, and only a small proportion of the goods are ever recovered, I'm afraid. Well, if you don't mind, I'll just check for fingerprints and any other clues. And if I were you, I'd get down to that letter straightaway.

8.8 TEXT BASED ON A VISUAL

Working in groups of two or three, look at the following eight photographs, and choose at least six of them. Arrange these in an order that makes a good story. Discuss the development of the story in the group, and invent any details that you need. Then, working individually, write the story.

8.9   IDEAS FOR STORIES

Choose one of the following topics, or any other topic that interests you.
    First, *write down in ten minutes as many ideas on the subject as you can.*
    Then *look through all the ideas, and decide if there are some that are not particularly important or relevant, and can therefore be left out.*
    After that, *group the ideas that you have, and decide on the best order, both within each group and among the groups.*
    Now *compose each paragraph, linking the ideas together with suitable words and phrases.*
    Finally, *bearing in mind the content of the whole story, write a suitable introduction and conclusion, if they are necessary to complete it.*

a) A story about a real or imaginary house or other building which has
    something mysterious about it.
b) The story of a competition in which you, or someone you know, took part.
c) The story of changing from one house or flat to another.
d) The outline of a film that you have seen, or a book that you have read.
e) The story of how you, or someone you know, managed to get a job that you
    (or he or she) really wanted.
f) The story of an unusual or difficult holiday or journey.
g) The story of a very special day: a visit, a birthday, a wedding, a hike, etc.
h) The story of a visit to someone in prison or in hospital.
i) The story of a burglary or robbery.
j) The story of a romance or love affair.

9 Business letters and memos

9.1 PUNCTUATION

Working in groups of two or three, punctuate the following letter, and decide where it should be divided into paragraphs. Then compare your answers with those of other groups.

dear sirs my recent order which arrived safely contained two items one Red Pyjama and one White Stripe Pyjama our daughter is four and a half months old weighs 7 kilos and is 61 centimetres long in other words she is a fairly average size for her age given this we were confident that the right size of pyjama for her would be the 70 cm which you claim will last until baby is some nine months old to our great disappointment the Red is a tight fit now while the White Stripe is a comfortable fit now and may last say one or two months misleading labelling and predictions are unfortunate in any circumstances but doubly so when the customer lives abroad apart from the trouble and cost of returning the things the fact is that our daughter needs the garments that we ordered now and we can thus hardly afford any delay could you please let me know whether it is your normal policy to overestimate the age and size for which a particular garment is suitable if this is so then we can simply take it into account when we make orders in the future I would like to point out that we are in general happy with your goods it is only the question of size which we find extremely irritating yours faithfully

Robin Purdue

Robin Purdue

9.2   SCRAMBLED SENTENCES

*The following sentences go together to form a complete memo, but they are in
the wrong order. Working in groups of two or three, put them in the right order,
and decide how the words and phrases underlined help to link the text together.
Then compare your answers with those of other groups.*

ROGERS HOLDINGS LTD   Memo

To: All staff   From: Company Secretary   Date: 12.3.82

a) To people outside the company he became even more famous when in 1979 he was
    awarded the OBE for services to British exports.

b) This absence was the first in thirty years of the Scheme's operation.

c) Unfortunately, this was unsuccessful, and he died peacefully in his sleep
    yesterday afternoon.

d) Moreover, work will stop at midday on Friday in order to give everybody the
    opportunity of attending Sir Clive's funeral.

e) Anyone with a personal family problem, for example, could always count on his
    sympathy and support.

f) It is with deep regret that I announce the death of our chairman,
    Sir Clive Rogers.

g) Only a few hours before, he had been reading the minutes of the last Staff
    Insurance Scheme meeting, which, owing to his illness, he was unable to attend.

h) Within the firm, on the other hand, he will be best remembered for his
    loyalty to, and his concern for, all members of his staff.

i) The Insurance Scheme, which was started by Sir Clive, was a typical product
    of his interest in his employees' wellbeing, and it justly made his name
    known far and wide.

j) I am sure, therefore, that all of you will join with me in sending condolences
    to his wife and family.

k) As many of you know, he had been ill for some time, and on Tuesday he under-
    went an emergency operation in the Southsex General Hospital.

F. T. Pratt.

9.3 LINKING WORDS AND PHRASES

In the following memo the linking words and phrases have been missed out.
Working in groups of two or three, choose the most appropriate word or phrase
from the ones given. Then compare your answers with those of other groups.

---

bst Bristol Small Tools

Memo from: General Manager   **To:** Managing Director

Date: 25 May 1982   **Ref No:** GRS/45/at

(1) .... we have agreed in principle to try and cut down
on staff, there are two serious problems in the Buying Department.

(2) ...., the clerk in charge of ordering from the stores
is also responsible for the filing of information. (3) ....,
at the end of the month, when most people want replacements from the
stores, and (4) .... require information from the files, he is
unable to keep up with the demand. (5) ...., he is practically
unoccupied during the first week of every month, when he could be
helping someone else, (6) .... I suggest we try to reorganise
his job.

(7) ...., the stores supervisor is getting rather old for
the job, and (8) ...., he is still suffering from the same old
complaint, (9) kleptomania. I (10) .... recommend that he be
invited to retire early, (11) .... we'll have no stores left!

(12) ...., if we were to appoint a much younger and more
qualified man to replace him, there would be several advantages over the
present arrangements. (13) ...., we could put him in charge
of his own ordering, and (14) .... reduce the burden on the
buying clerk. We might (15) .... ask him to take a more active
part than his predecessor in the annual stocktaking.

I would argue, (16) ...., that we approach the union, and
suggest that Higgins should be retired early, and (17) ....,
that his job should be upgraded to Clerical Grade G7. (18) ....,
we could ask the Personnel Department to draw up a new job specification
on these lines.

---

1 a) In spite of   b) While   c) Because
2 a) Firstly   b) At first   c) Namely
3 a) So that   b) Consequently
   c) Because
4 a) also   b) on the other hand
   c) therefore
5 a) Also   b) In contrast   c) Otherwise
6 a) so   b) although   c) but
7 a) Consequently   b) Secondly
   c) After all
8 a) thirdly   b) on the contrary
   c) furthermore
9 a) for example   b) also   c) i.e.

10 a) therefore   b) so   c) also
11 a) if not   b) otherwise
   c) consequently
12 a) For example   b) Therefore
   c) Now
13 a) E.g.   b) Namely   c) For instance
14 a) thus   b) in the same way
   c) similarly
15 a) also   b) secondly   c) too
16 a) finally   b) therefore   c) at last
17 a) consequently   b) moreover   c) then
18 a) In spite of this   b) Meanwhile
   c) Therefore

9.4 REPORTING WORDS

There are two reported speech versions of the following direct speech. Working in groups of two or three, decide which you prefer, and why. In particular consider the role of the reporting words admit *and* promise. *Then discuss your conclusion with other groups.*

'O.K., we made a small mistake in the calculations,' Mrs Clare said to her assistant, 'but they don't have to get so worked up about it. In any case, we'll get the revised figures to them by the end of the week.'

a) Mrs Clare admitted that a small mistake was made, but she promised that the revised figures would arrive by the end of the week.
b) Mrs Clare said that O.K. they had made a small mistake in the calculations, but that they didn't have to get so worked up about it. She said that in any case they would get the revised figures to them by the end of the week.

Now report the following items of direct speech, choosing in each case one of the pairs of reporting words given. Then compare your answers with those of others.

think, propose;   assume, invite;   greet, ask;   deny, suggest;   complain, threaten;   explain, propose;   thank, offer;   insist, warn;   call, advise;   refuse, insist;   promise, invite;   apologise, forgive.

1 'They must have had time to read the report by now,' said the chief engineer. 'I've sent a telegram to their design bloke asking for his comments.'
2 'Mr Winterbottom,' said the mayor's assistant, 'under no circumstances will you be allowed to see the mayor. For the last time I'm asking you to leave this office at once.'
3 'I've told those people in Stockport before, and I tell them again,' the works manager said. 'There's definitely something wrong with the gauges.' Then he added, 'They're crazy if they use that machine before it's been properly serviced.'
4 'I give you my word,' said the manageress, 'that I won't tell anyone what you say, Mr Ridgeway, but I really would be pleased if you could put down your comments on paper and let me have them.'
5 'What they say about us overcharging them is nonsense,' said the accountant. 'What they ought to do is to compare our prices with those of our competitors.'
6 'Good morning, Thomson,' said the director. 'I'm glad to see you're back at work again. Is there any post for me?'

Now choose two or three of the pairs of reporting words that you have not so far used; write examples of direct speech and reported speech to illustrate the use of these words.

9.5   FIRST AND LAST PARAGRAPHS

The following is a memo which consists of three paragraphs, of which the second and third are given. Working in groups of two or three, decide which of the suggestions makes the most suitable first paragraph. Then discuss your answer with other groups.

Grove, Briggs & Co Ltd

TO: all staff   3.11.1982

Choices for first paragraph:

a) Mrs Scott has worked for the company for almost 15 years and, as everybody knows, she is our Marketing Director, although that is the result of a fairly recent promotion. She is an excellent planner, and has been particularly successful with campaigns involving newspaper and magazine advertising.

b) A marketing meeting was held on 28.10.1982; those present were A G Grove, Chairman; B S Daniels, Managing Director; Mrs J B Scott, Marketing Director; and S Holmes, Company Secretary. The purpose of the meeting was to consider the plans prepared by the Marketing Director for the launching of our latest product, the skin cream Bumsmooth.

c) Bumsmooth is our latest product, and everybody connected with its production, including myself, is proud of it and hopeful that it will sell as well as some of our other new products. There are similar creams on sale in Germany and France, but we will be the first to market such a product in this country.

    Mrs Scott's plans for Bumsmooth have been prepared with two alternatives in mind: the first is a campaign based mainly on newspaper and magazine advertising, but with some TV back-up; the second is based on TV advertising plus brochures delivered to individual homes. The second alternative was prepared in view of the threatened strike by newspaper printing staff. Although the printers have now in principle accepted an offer that was recently made, those present still felt that both alternatives should be considered.

    When all aspects had been reviewed, and costs compared, there was a unanimous decision to go ahead with the second alternative. In order to carry out the house-to-house distribution of the brochures in our own area, we are now looking for about 25 people, either from inside or outside the company, who are prepared to spend the weekends of 3-4 and 10-11 January in this work. Those interested should contact Mrs Scott direct on extension 346.

B S Daniels

The following are the second and third paragraphs of a business letter. Working individually, write a suitable first paragraph. Then compare your version with those of others.

(First paragraph missing)

```
   First, you do not mention the questions of transport and
insurance.  Are we to assume that you accept responsibility
for these, and that your quoted price includes the cost?
If not, could you let us know what your normal way of deal-
ing with these points is, and what the cost is likely to
be?

   Second, we find your letter somewhat vague as to the
delivery dates.  You mention that there may be strikes which
are beyond your control.  With respect, they are even less
within our control, and we would like to see an undertaking
that you accept responsibility at least for any possible
strikes among your own staff.

We look forward to hearing from you on both these points.
```

The following is a memo which consists of three paragraphs, of which the first and second are given. Working in groups of two or three, decide which of the suggestions makes the most suitable last paragraph. Then discuss your answer with those of other groups.

Britplast Co Ltd
Norton Street
Rotherham

```
Memo to Directors and all Sales, Finance and Scientific staff
                                              30.5.1982

Report and Recommendations based on experiences at
The British Homes Exhibition, Earls Court, London

The size of our stand at this year's exhibition was the same as it
has been for the last seven years, namely 700 square feet (35 feet
long by 20 feet deep).  It was staffed by various people during the
10 days of the exhibition, but mostly our representatives were from
the sales and finance departments, including at times me and/or
Mr Sallis, the Finance Director.

In recent years two important developments have taken place in the
plastic container industry.  One is that the competition, especially
from foreign companies, has grown considerably, and several stands
were larger and better staffed than ours.  Second, our customers
and potential customers are increasingly demanding - as happened on
several occasions during this exhibition - technical details and
specifications which the people on our stand were unable to supply.
```

⋙⟶

a) There were four German and three Japanese stands of 1,000 square feet or more, and even some of our British competitors had very interesting stands, which made ours look not quite so attractive as it has been in the past. Since we were all in the same area, it was quite easy to see the effect on potential customers and it certainly made us think.

b) I would therefore like to make two suggestions, which should be considered with a view to making our presence more effective at future exhibitions. First, the stand should be larger so as to give greater impact and to keep up with our competitors. Second, the staffing should always include at least one of our scientists, preferably a senior one, so that we can give on-the-spot advice to our potential customers. I would be pleased to hear reactions to these suggestions.

c) It is true, of course, that we have so far maintained our proportion of the market, and our total sales have in fact risen slightly in each of the last seven years, i.e. during the time that we have had the present type of stand at the exhibition. But we cannot simply hope that these things will continue, and we must think of the future.

James D Proctor
Sales Director

The following are the first and the second paragraphs of a report. Write a suitable third (concluding) paragraph.

Englang (Publishers) Ltd

Memo to : Directors, and all Sales, Finance and Editorial Staff

Report and Recommendations based on our Experiences at the recent International Book Fair, Frankfurt.

This year was the sixth successive time that we have been represented at the annual Frankfurt Fair. We have always felt that it is useful in a general way to attend, to display a representative sample of our books, and - not least - to have a look at what other publishers, both British and foreign, are producing. Our stand has always been 45 square metres and is staffed mainly by our marketing personnel.

Over the last few years the fastest rising area of book production has been in materials for teaching English to foreigners, and five years ago we decided to enter this field in a more determined fashion. Since then we have brought out some interesting material, both for students and for teachers, but the stand did not have room to display all of these titles, nor were our marketing staff able to cope with all the specific and detailed questions raised by visiting teachers, inspectors, and so on.

(Third paragraph missing)

Robert Regent,
Marketing Manager.

9.6   TEXT COMPARISON

Working in groups of two or three, decide which of the following letters you prefer, and why. Then discuss your decision with other groups. Finally, rewrite the letter you did not like.

Briggs Manufacturing Co Ltd
Harvey Street
Leadstone
LS12 8HG

26 Scarr Avenue
Nottington
NT4 5BG

26 October 1982

Dear Sirs,

I would like to apply for the post of office manager which you advertised in the Guardian of 24 October 1982. I feel that I am the right sort of person for the post because my qualifications and experience are extremely appropriate.

I was born in 1948, and I went to school in Nottington from 1953 to 1965. I left school with the General Certificate of Education, with good grades in Maths, English and French. I have since attended Nottington Polytechnic to study company law, accounting, industrial psychology, and other subjects related to modern office work. I received the Diploma in Office Studies in 1969.

After leaving school I joined Port and Starbud as a junior clerk. When I received my Diploma, I felt it was time for a change and I became a senior clerk with Bolton and Ward. I have been working as Assistant Manager there since my promotion in 1974.

I enjoy all aspects of office supervision, and I believe that I now have the right combination of youth and experience to accept a new challenge. Moreover, I am certain that my present employers would give me excellent references. I therefore hope that you will give my application the serious consideration which I feel it deserves.

Yours faithfully,

Irene Brown

(Mrs) Irene Brown.

---

43 Southway Lane,
Emsley.
TY3 4DY

27 October 1982

Dear Sirs,

I think I am the right person for the job because I have the right qualifications, and they gave me promotion because they like my work. Also I have the right experience. The advertisement was in The Guardian of 22 October 1982. I think you should consider my application seriously. I went to school from 1950 to 1965. I have the General Certificate of Education and I have studied Fibre Technology and Colour Chemistry, but that was not at school. It was at Bristol Technical College, but at school I got good grades in Maths, Physics and Chemistry when I took the Certificate in 1964. Your advertisement was for a works manager. Then I studied the other subjects related to textile manufacture. I was given promotion and I have been Assistant Works Manager since 1978. I like my work very much and I have a Diploma in Textiles from Bristol Technical College. That was in 1968. I was born in 1945, and I worked for the Topp Clothing Company from 1968 to 1973. I am prepared to work hard and I am sure that Prior Productions would give me an excellent reference.

Yours faithfully,

Colin Whitfield

(Mr.) Colin Whitfield.

Terry Textiles,
Brighouse Lane,
Wandsthorpe.
W7 4HP

9.7   TEXT BASED ON A VISUAL

The Warehouse Supervisor sent the following memo and the accompanying plan to the General Manager. The Manager has jotted his comments and ideas on the plan. Working in groups of two or three, decide on the Manager's reply, and then write it. Compare your version with that of other groups.

Hornby & Sons
Special Steels

Memo from: A. J. George   To: G. Bennett

I wish to bring to your attention the inadequacy of the existing facilities for washing and changing for warehouse staff. At present there are 35 men and women employed in various parts of the warehouse. In the course of their everyday work they are normally exposed to dust, dirt and oil. It is therefore desirable that they should be able to shower and change in reasonable comfort at the conclusion of their day's work.

The only available space at the moment is very cramped. There is no proper provision for hanging up, storing and drying clothes, and there is only one wash-basin, which is cracked and coming away from the wall. There is no hot water. The Factories Act (1961) Part 3, Section 58, requires that adequate and suitable facilities for washing including hot water, soap and clean towels should be provided. The Ministry of Labour's notes to the Act also strongly recommend separate facilities for men and women, especially if large numbers of people are involved.

As I see it, the following alternatives could be considered:

a)   The building of a new amenity block on the empty site of the old canteen, to contain showers, washbasins, a changing area with clothes lockers, and a space for drying clothes.

b)   Extension and improvement of the existing arrangements, by dedicating a portion of the present storage space to showers and a locker room.

c)   Continuation of the present facilities here, but with the staff changing elsewhere.

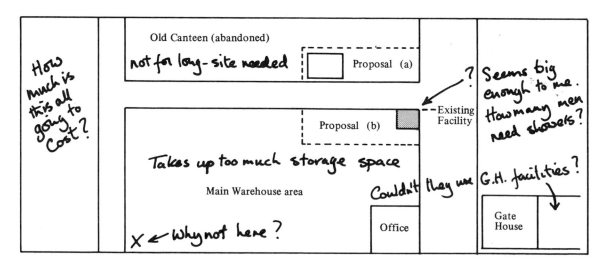

9.8 IDEAS FOR LETTERS AND MEMOS

Choose one of the following topics, or any other topic that interests you.
   First, *write down in ten minutes as many ideas as you can on the subject.*
   Then *look through the ideas, and decide if there are some that are not particularly important or relevant, and can therefore be left out.*
   After that, *group the ideas that you have, and decide on the best order, both within each group and among the groups.*
   Now *compose each paragraph, linking the ideas together with suitable words and phrases.*
   Finally, *bearing in mind the content of the whole letter or memo, write a suitable introduction and also a suitable conclusion.*

a) A reply to the letter in 9.1, accepting responsibility, giving explanations, and offering to exchange the goods.
b) A reply to the letter in 9.1, declining to accept responsibility, and giving the reasons for this.
c) A memo on the death of a woman who started in a company as a cleaner, and gradually worked her way up to more and more influential positions; she always fought for women's rights, both inside the firm and outside. (Compare 9.2.)
d) A reply to the memo of 9.3, accepting part and rejecting part, and making alternative suggestions.
e) A memo to all the staff of a large company, suggesting ways of economising on the use of paper, electricity, etc.
f) A reply to the second letter in 9.5, taking up each of the points and reassuring the potential client.

23rd — 30 — 7th

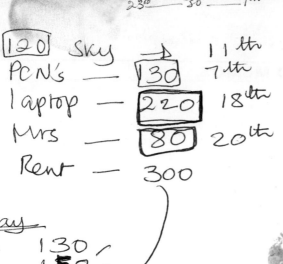

120 Sky → 11th
PCN's — 130 7th
laptop — 220 18th
Mrs — 80 20th
Rent — 300

260

Tday
Shoes 130
C/T 158

Jse + ac
Chard + ac

- Reply to PCN
- Brent Rub call
- CTC exps (Send)
- letters.